SANTIAGO CALATRAVA

SANTIAGO CALATRAVA

Structure and Expression

MATILDA McQUAID

THE MUSEUM OF MODERN ART, NEW YORK
Distributed by Harry N. Abrams, Inc., New York

Published on the occasion of the exhibition *Santiago Calatrava: Structure and Expression*,
March 25–May 18, 1993, organized by Matilda McQuaid, Assistant Curator,
Department of Architecture and Design, The Museum of Modern Art, New York

This publication is made possible by a generous grant from the Government of Valencia, Spain.

Produced by the Department of Publications
The Museum of Modern Art, New York
Osa Brown, Director
Edited by Alexandra Bonfante-Warren
Designed by Jody Hanson
Production by Marc Sapir
Printed and bound by Herlin Press Inc., West Haven, CT

Library of Congress Catalog Card Number 93-77206

All sketches by Santiago Calatrava

ISBN 0-87070-164-9 (MoMA)
ISBN 0-8109-6128-8 (Abrams)

Printed in the United States of America
Published by The Museum of Modern Art
11 West 53 Street, New York, N.Y. 10019

Distributed in the United States and Canada by Harry N. Abrams, Inc., New York. A Times Mirror Company

Distributed outside the United States and Canada by Thames and Hudson, London

PHOTOGRAPHY CREDITS

The Museum of Modern Art, New York, Department of Architecture and Design: photo: John Edward Linden, London: front cover, 18 bottom, 39 top left, back cover; photo: Ellen Grossman, New York: frontispiece, 8, 19 bottom left and right, 22 left top, center, and bottom, 24 right top and center, 26 top, 27 top, 28 top, 29 top and center, 30 top right and left, 31 top left to right, 32, 33 bottom, 35 top and center, 37 top left and center left, 38 bottom, 39 top center; photo: Mischol, Schiers, Switzerland: 9; 10 top; photo: Oscar Savio, Rome: 10 bottom; photo: Erwin Lang, Los Angeles: 11; photo: copyright Paolo Rosselli, Milan: 12 top right, 16, 17 bottom left, 17 bottom right, 20 top, 22 right, 23 top left, 23 bottom, 24 top left, 25 left center and bottom, and top right, 36 top, 37 top right, 37 right center, 38 top, 39 top right, 39 bottom left; from *Il Codice Atlantico di Leonardo da Vinci* [Facsimile of the restored manuscript in the Biblioteca Ambrosiana, Milan] (Florence: Gaspare Barbera: Giunti; New York: Johnson Reprint, Harcourt Brace Jovanovich, ©1973, 1975), fol. 844r, Courtesy Avery Architectural and Fine Arts Library, Columbia University in the City of New York, photo: Heinrich Helfenstein, Zurich: 12 top left; photo: Frei Otto, Berlin: 13 top right; photo: Heinrich Helfenstein, Zurich: 12 bottom, 13 center right; photo: Clemens Kalischer, Stockbridge, MA: 14 top left and right; 15; courtesy of Santiago Calatrava Valls: 17 top, center, and left top, 18 top, 19 top left to right, 20 bottom, 21, 23 top right, 24 left bottom, 25 top left and bottom right, 26 bottom, 27 bottom, 28 bottom, 29 bottom, 30 bottom left and right, 31 right center and bottom, 32 top, 34, 35 bottom, 36 bottom, 37 left center and bottom, 39 left center and right center and bottom; photo: Kate Keller: 24 right bottom.

Front cover: Kuwait Pavilion, 1992 World's Fair. 1991–92. Seville

Back cover: Alamillo Bridge and Cartuga Viaduct. 1987–92. Seville

Frontispiece: Santiago Calatrava. Sketch for the Cathedral of Saint John the Divine, René Dubos bioshelter (project). 1991. Pen and ink on paper, 9½ x 7" (24.1 x 17.8 cm)

Inside front and back covers: Santiago Calatrava. Preliminary sketches for Stadelhofen Railroad Station, train platform and entrance to underpass. c. 1983. Pencil and colored pencil on trace, 11⅞ x 24¾" (30.2 x 53.5 cm)

CONTENTS

FOREWORD

This survey of selected works of Santiago Calatrava is the first of a series of exhibitions presenting significant developments in contemporary architecture. Thresholds in Contemporary Architecture will focus on themes and issues in recent work, in the form of monographic exhibitions, as well as other formats, rather than on broad retrospective assessments. The series will identify designers whose work is innovative and also promises important future developments.

Santiago Calatrava: Structure and Expression is a particularly appropriate exhibition to inaugurate this series. Throughout most of this century the practitioners of architecture and engineering have been sharply divided: the architect has been the designer, the engineer has been consultant and analyst. Calatrava's work in the last decade, however, has successfully transcended these boundaries, redefining the relationship between architect and engineer and between their respective disciplines. Perhaps more than any other, he has helped to revive the role of engineer as proactive designer, in the tradition of John Augustus Roebling, Alexandre-Gustave Eiffel, and, more recently, as Matilda McQuaid discusses, Robert Maillart, Pier Luigi Nervi, Eduardo Torroja, and Felix Candela.

Just as importantly, Calatrava's exuberant designs for civic commissions have reinvigorated the concept of public works as meaningful symbols of urban pride. Given the frequent hostility of modern architects toward the symbols and structure of the traditional city—as expressed in both Le Corbusier's Plan Voisin and Frank Lloyd Wright's Broadacre City project—the revival of public works on a heroic scale is remarkable. That they have been received so enthusiastically is also noteworthy, indicating the extent of the public's need for meaningful expressions of communal effort.

As the conditions of American urban life once again surface on this nation's political agenda, so too will the construction and reconstruction of public works. Santiago Calatrava's contributions to the increase of the public realm, the intuitive power and urbanity of his structures, should be well noted in planning for the revitalization of our cities' infrastructures.

Terence Riley
Director
Department of Architecture and Design

ACKNOWLEDGMENTS

On behalf of The Museum of Modern Art I would like to thank the sponsors who made enormous commitments to the various parts of the exhibition: for their very generous support of the exhibition, catalogue, and the special installation of tree structures at the entrance to the exhibition, the Government of Valencia, Spain, and in particular Mr. Joan Lerma I Blasco, president of the Generalitat Valenciana. I am also indebted to Mr. Thomas Schmidheiny for underwriting the fabrication and installation of the sculpture *Machine for Making Shadows*, in the Abby Aldrich Rockefeller Sculpture Garden. I am especially grateful for Robertina Calatrava's efforts toward securing the support for the exhibition.

Without the cooperation of the Santiago Calatrava Valls office, this exhibition would have been impossible to put together. I would especially like to thank Anthony Tischhauser for his patience and for his ability to answer all of my questions at times when he was juggling many other projects in the office. Others in the office who provided help were: José Luis Moro, Kim Marangoni, Frank Lorino, Annilie Morvay, and Grazyna Huk. I am indebted to Santiago Calatrava, who demonstrated complete confidence, tremendous generosity, and general enthusiasm throughout the preparation of this exhibition. I am truly grateful to him and his work. His modelmakers, Zaborowsky Models, have created outstanding representations of Calatrava's work, and the photographers Heinrich Helfenstein, John Edward Linden, Paolo Rosselli, and Ellen Grossman have been extremely helpful and forthcoming with the beautiful photographs included in this publication.

At the Museum, I would like to thank James S. Snyder, Deputy Director for Planning and Program Support, and Kirk Varnedoe, Director, Department of Painting and Sculpture, for graciously permitting the special installation in the Sculpture Garden. Eleni Cocordas, Associate Coordinator of Exhibitions, provided invaluable support in organizing a complicated budget and advising on so many areas of the exhibition. The Department of Publications has contributed an abundance of enthusiasm and support. My special thanks to Osa Brown, Director; Harriet Bee, Managing Editor; Nancy Kranz, Manager of Promotion and Special Services; and Tim McDonough, Production Manager, who all saw the potential of Calatrava's work; to Alexandra Bonfante-Warren, who clarified my thoughts and writing and showed enormous devotion to the project; and to Marc Sapir, whose admirable production skills kept us all on schedule. In the Department of Graphics, I relied on Assistant Director Jody Hanson's wonderful design ability to interpret my thoughts and Calatrava's work, resulting in this very handsome publication. I would like to thank the Department of Public Information, particularly Helen Bennett, Press Representative, for their publicity efforts; Sarah Stephenson, Education Center Program Coordinator, and Romy Phillips, Programs Coordinator, in the Department of Education for their installation assistance in the Edward John Noble Education Center; John Wielk, Manager of Exhibition and Project Funding, Development Department; and Nestor Montilla, Assistant Registrar, in the Registrar's Department; Exhibition Production and Design, directed by Jerome Neuner has, as always, done a superb job of organizing a complicated installation, and I am very grateful to Douglas Feick, Production Supervisor, for his magnanimous efforts and quick responses to my numerous requests.

In the Department of Architecture and Design, Terence Riley, Director, has been extremely supportive and offered me valuable criticism on my essay, and Assistant Curator Peter Reed's intelligent comments about the essay were also welcome. Anne Dixon, Study Center Supervisor, was indispensable in the planning stages and installation of the exhibition, and provided me with important insights and limitless support. Jennifer Brody, Assistant to the Director, and Timothy Rohan, Executive Secretary, have, as usual, managed effortlessly and very well many of the technical aspects of the exhibition.

I would like to thank Cara McCarty, Guy Nordenson, and Anthony Webster, who all generously offered their time as outside readers; my essay has benefited from their input. Finally, my gratitude to Craig Konyk, who not only collaborated on the installation design but has been an articulate critic and tireless listener.

M.M.

Santiago Calatrava. Sketches for Valencia Planetarium. 1992. Pencil and watercolor on paper, 8 x 10 1/2" (20.3 x 26.7 cm)

SANTIAGO CALATRAVA

Structure and Expression

MATILDA McQUAID

It is not enough to be an engineer. We are not allowed to confine ourselves within our own professions, but must live in full view of the entire scene of life, which is always total. The supreme art of living is a consummation gained by no single calling and no single science; it is the yield of all occupations and all sciences, and many things besides.

—José Ortega y Gasset,
"Man the Technician"

Human endeavors are enriched by an intuitive vision that draws on all experienced and studied phenomena. As much as structural theory and geometry, this can inspire monumental works of architecture. Such a belief underlies the work of the Spanish architect and engineer Santiago Calatrava (b. 1951), whose expressive use of technology and inventive form would be impossible without an awareness that goes beyond architecture and engineering. Music, painting, and the natural sciences are as vital to his work as any calculation. The landscaped structures that he creates evoke an empathic response, reaffirming a place for awe in the criteria for building.

Calatrava is part of the distinguished heritage of twentieth-century engineering. Like those of the preceding generations—Robert Maillart, Pier Luigi Nervi, Eduardo Torroja, and Felix Candela—Calatrava goes beyond an approach that merely solves technical problems. Structure, for these engineers, is a balance between the scientific criterion of efficien-

Robert Maillart. Salginatobel Bridge. 1930. Canton Grisons, Switzerland

cy and the innovation of new forms. Calatrava considers engineering "the art of the possible,"[1] and seeks a new vocabulary of form that is based on technical know-how, yet is not an anthem to techniques.[2]

Maillart was one of the first engineers of this century to break completely from masonry construction and apply a technically appropriate and elegant solution to reinforced concrete construction. Although the technical idea in Calatrava's work is neither the primary motivation, as with Maillart, nor understated, it informs the overall expression of the structure. His work becomes an "intertwinement of plastic expression and structural revelation, producing results that possibly can be best described as a synthesis of aesthetics and structural physics."[3]

For Torroja, Nervi, and Candela, a structural work of art derived equally from aesthetic choices, the creative imagination, and science. Torroja recognized that good structural design evolves only when its concerns go beyond science and techniques to include "art, common sense, sentiment, aptitude and joy in creating pleasing outlines."[4] Nervi, like Maillart, designed his works to be pleasing visually but also financially economical and efficient in construction. The modern design principles of efficiency, economy, and beauty became interdependent in his technical process, producing results such as the elegant roof pattern in the Palazzetto dello Sport (1957) in Rome.

Top: Eduardo Torroja. Technical Institute of Construction and Cement. Pergola frames. 1951. Costillares, Spain

Above: Pier Luigi Nervi with Annibale Vitellozzi. Palazzetto dello Sport. 1957. Rome

Candela, who is Calatrava's close friend and mentor, draws on his experience as a builder to construct the thinnest conceivable shell. Candela created a variety of structures that used the hyperbolic paraboloid, or saddle-shaped shell, which was stiffer and easier to build than other shell constructions. The Iglesia de la Virgen Milagrosa, in Navarte, Mexico, which was completed in 1955, represents the incredible virtuosity with which he was able to manipulate this form into thin concrete shell roofs and walls. Hyperbolic paraboloids constitute the entire structure, including the walls and roof. They suggest Gothic space, but are clearly rooted in modern design principles.

Like many twentieth-century engineers, Calatrava considers concrete to be the most noble construction material. The Spanish word for concrete, *hormigon*, from the word meaning "form," describes most directly the unique quality of this building material—its ability to take any form. But Calatrava does not limit himself to concrete; the dialogue he establishes between concrete and steel, for example, and the detailing of these connections reveal a great deal about his ideas on structural composition. In the Bach de Roda–Felipe II Bridge (1984–87) (pp. 36–37), in Barcelona, the arches are transformed from steel into concrete as they bend to meet the earth. Concrete abutments are anchored firmly on the ground, while steel—because of its appar-

Felix Candela. Iglesia de la Virgen Milagrosa. 1954–55. Navarte, Mexico

ent lightness—soars over the roadway. The three-pronged steel columns in Zurich's Stadelhofen Railroad Station (1983–90) (pp. 24–25) seem to bite into the glass canopy and concrete promenade to ensure support and grip. These junctures embody Calatrava's fascination with the way loads are carried to the ground.

Calatrava's design process reflects his eclectic education. Beginning as an art student in his birthplace of Valencia, he earned a degree in architecture from the Escuela Technica Superior de Arquitectura de Valencia and a doctorate of technical science from the Eidgenosische Technische Hochschule (ETH) in Zurich. Frequently he makes numerous sketches, working out the design and the technical requirements simultaneously. These sketches emphasize his preference for resolving a design in section, which for Calatrava reveals not only the strength of the building but also its structural beauty.

Natural images—the profile of a charging bull, the various contortions of the human body, studies of trees—are juxtaposed to and interspersed with sketches of his current projects: bridges, stations, pavilions, and others. This fascination with organic and anatomical relationships is integrated into his built projects, such as the Science Museum, Planetarium, and Telecommunications Tower in Valencia (1991–) (pp. 32–35), or Stadelhofen, where the repeated structural elements over the promenade canopy look like the ribcage of a stegosaurus.

Sketches are sometimes followed by scale models—or what Calatrava refers to as "toys and games."[5] Used as experiments and primarily inspirational tools for resolving a technical problem, such as dynamics or tension, they can also be seen as sculptures that borrow the language of engineering. They are creative statements about structural forces.

Calatrava's comprehension of science and technical information allows his work a creative starting point that recalls Leonardo da Vinci's own interconnected scientific and artistic explorations. If Leonardo's art made use of his scientific knowledge and of the automatisms that characterized his machines, these in turn depended on his artistic capacity to capture the animation that characterizes the universe.[6] By observing human and animal anatomy, Leonardo was able to translate human and animal movement into mechanical motion.

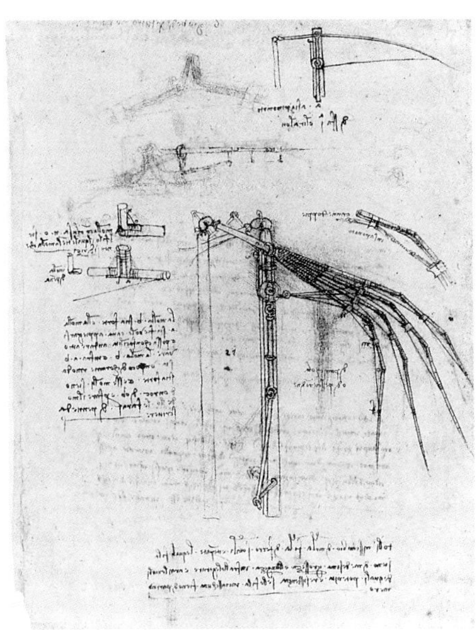

Leonardo da Vinci. Study of a wing mechanism for a flying machine. c. 1493–95

Santiago Calatrava. Swissbau Pavilion. 1989. Basel

Calatrava's passion for machines and technology is revealed in the Swissbau Pavilion (1989) in Basel, which he describes as "a machine for making shadows."[7] Exploiting the sculptural quality of reinforced concrete and its little-considered ability to act as the primary material for a mechanism, this pavilion represents the first in a series of projects exploring the idea of kinetic architectural components. The other projects—the unbuilt floating concrete pavilion on the Lake of Lucerne (1990), the Planetarium in Valencia, and the Kuwait Pavilion (1991–92) (pp. 18–19) in Seville—celebrate motion and light with roofs that move.

Santiago Calatrava. *Toros.* 1985. Wood and stainless-steel wire

Movement has always fascinated Calatrava and has been a source of inspiration and evolution for parts of his structures. Even in his engineering thesis on foldable space frames, he investigated movement as an inherent part of architecture, concluding that a building is not just a visual image made up of different volumes and textured surfaces but a dynamic object.

Some of his structures, like the projects discussed above, literally move, while others, such as Lyons Airport Railroad Station (1989–) (pp. 20–23), the addition to the Cathedral of Saint John the Divine (1991–) (pp. 30–31) in New York City, and Stadelhofen, depict crystallized movement. Lyons Airport Railroad Station, which functions as a terminal for both regional and fast-through trains to the airport, echoes Eero Saarinen's TWA Terminal at Kennedy Airport (1957–62) in its suggestion of a bird in flight. Just as Eadweard Muybridge depicted man in motion and motion as form in his late-nineteenth-century photographs, Calatrava gives form to speed in the sweeping curve of the tracks at Stadelhofen. The series of four bridges that connect the park-like hillside and the center of the city reinforces this sense of movement as one crosses to the promenade above or the station below. The dramatic slope of the main bridge elicits arms spread open and an all-out race across to the other side. The station becomes a clear and purposeful incision into the central part of Zurich, connecting the old with the new and creating a work of revitalized urban vision.

In his bioshelter—an artificial environment for plant life that comprises his addition to Saint John the Divine—and in his Alamillo Bridge and Cartuga Viaduct in Seville (1987–92) (pp. 38–39), movement is represented by the tension that is inherent when proportions are exaggerated or attenuated. These structures perform almost like trained athletes, who jump and hurl and balance themselves without apparent effort. One admires Calatrava's own soaring space in the cathedral and the flying buttresses that resist the forces of gravity. The Alamillo Bridge, a commission in honor of the 1992 World's Fair in Seville, is dominated by a massive pylon that rises at a 58-degree angle and counteracts the pull of the cable stays. Calatrava has created a dynamic composition that is both a gateway and a civic monument to the city of Seville.

Frei Otto. Tree Structures (project), Yale University. 1960. New Haven

Although nature is Calatrava's structural inspiration, he does not imitate any particular organic form. Instead, he observes the strong visual movement in natural objects that derives from the fact that their shapes are the traces of the physical forces that created them. His structures have the same dynamic quality emphasized in Rudolf Arnheim's explanation of nature. It is "alive to our eyes partly because its shapes are fossils of the events that gave rise to them."[8]

The organic forms and dramatic spatial qualities of Calatrava's architecture were the most appropriate choice for the winning scheme for an addition to Saint John the Divine. In the Gothic cathedral, which celebrated its centennial in 1992, flying buttresses, pointed arches, and structural tracery enclose and support a glass-skinned bioshelter above the nave, creating a lyrical structure that joins the spiritual and the ecological, heaven and earth. One can imagine Calatrava's completed cathedral devoted to the elements of light and space, mystical and powerful in their inspiration.

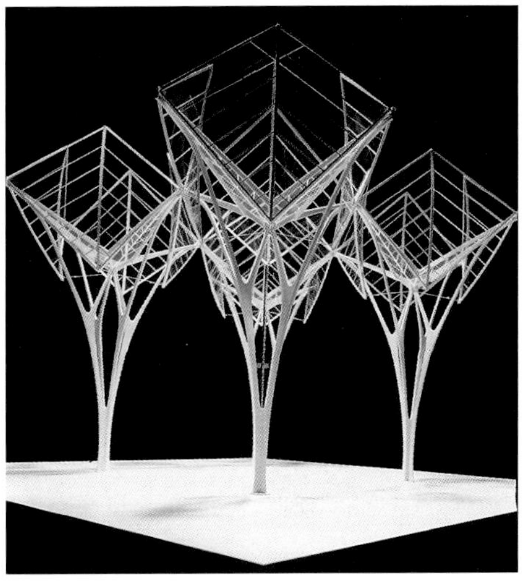

Santiago Calatrava. Restaurant Bauschänzli (project). 1988. Zurich

Possibly Calatrava's closest link to nature is his interpretation and use of the tree form. It is a historical motif that has also inspired some of the major architects and engineers of the twentieth century—Frank Lloyd Wright, Nervi, Maillart, Frei Otto. They have chosen this form not

Rudolf Steiner. Second Goetheanum. 1924–28. Dornach, Switzerland

only because, as a column, it counteracts the thrusts of arches and domes and supports the weight of massive stone construction, but also because it conveys structural clarity and rhythmic qualities. In his project for Spandau Railroad Station (1991) (pp. 26–29), in Berlin, Calatrava allows the park across the street to enter the site of the station. Inside, he represents the tree in abstracted form, which functions as a structural support for the glazed roof over the train platform. With this gesture he creates a direct link with the city, transforming the canopy of trees into a canopy of structure.

The most direct and dramatic example is in Saint John the Divine, where the tree is the structural metaphor for the cathedral. An interpretation of the tripartite section as foliage (roof), trunk (nave), and roots (crypt) is reflected in one of Calatrava's first sketches for the cathedral. The aboretum above the nave allows the tree a literal representation and creates a living stained-glass window.

The process of transformation, whether physical or metaphysical, that is present in Calatrava's work reminds one of the heritage he shares with Spanish artists like Francisco Goya, Salvador Dalí, Joan Miró, and Antoni Gaudi. The visionary and mystical quality of Goya's work is echoed over a century later by Dalí in his dream-like paintings and in the architecture of Gaudi, who expressed fundamental architectonic principles with wild lyricism. Miró's biomorphic abstractions seem to change before our eyes, expanding and contracting like single-cell organisms.

The process by which Calatrava transforms the tree itself recalls Rudolf Steiner's Goetheanum (1913–22, destroyed by fire; second constructed 1924–28) in Dornach, Switzerland. Steiner relied on Goethe's principle of plant metamorphosis, according to which the qualities of any form in the growth sequence are prefigured in the previous form and continue to some degree in the succeeding shape. Goethe described a plant as primarily a leaf that metamorphoses through an ordered process of expansion and contraction to become also a seed, a pod, a blossom, and a fruit.[9] Steiner introduced the "principle of metamorphosis into organic architecture . . . to move from the static conception of [a trabeated] system to the active principle of growth, wherein one form emerges from another in a variety of ways."[10]

There is another similarity between Steiner and Calatrava that relates to Steiner's principle of the living wall. Walls are not intended merely for containment but are sculptural surfaces that are able to communicate mobility and penetrability. Steiner pointed to the earth, with its covering of plant life, as a model for the living wall.[11] When one looks at Calatrava's Ernsting's Warehouse (1983–85) (pp. 16–17), in Coesfeld, Germany, it is clear that architecture is not static. The warehouse doors continue the aluminum wall surface when closed, but when they open, the facade is pierced and set in motion and the doors are transformed into a beautiful scalloped canopy. In Stadelhofen, the billowing walls of the upper promenade seem to come alive as the steel pergola casts its shadows. The lower commercial level is a gallery of concrete sculpture, as series of arches span the passageway, while others form unexpected twists and knots. Such dynamic forms also recall Gaudi's Park Güell (1900–14) in Barcelona, where rubble columns emulating slanting tree trunks create a colonnade, and entire wall surfaces are animated by mosaics and seem to be hollowed out by waves. Gaudi's park becomes both a petrified forest underneath and a magical resting spot above.

Antoni Gaudi. Park Güell. Colonnade. 1900–14. Barcelona

Calatrava's work can captivate, communicate, and inspire through a visual process. We sense a familiarity with it that is often definable yet not attributable to a single source. One imagines elements of his bridges and railroad stations in a natural history museum as easily as in their urban context. At a time of increasing specialization in architecture, Calatrava combines the disciplines of architecture and engineering with his own creative vision. It is a vision that has the potential to rejuvenate not only the built environment but ultimately the very spirit of building itself.

NOTES

1. Conversation with the author, December 1992.
2. *El Croquis, De arquitectura y de diseño* 38 (March 1989): 6.
3. Anthony C. Webster, "Utility, Technology and Expression," *The Architectural Review* 191, no. 1149 (November 1992): 71.
4. Eduardo Torroja, "Notes on Structural Expression," *Art and Artist* (Berkeley and Los Angeles: University of California Press, 1956), p. 220.
5. Santiago Calatrava, "The Synthetic Power of Games and Metaphor." In *Bridging the Gap: Rethinking the Relationship of Architect and Engineer* (New York: Van Nostrand Reinhold, Building Arts Forum/New York, 1991), p. 173.
6. Marco Cianchi, *Leonardo da Vinci's Machines* (Florence: Becocci Editore, 1988), p. 16.
7. Conversation with the author, July 1992.
8. Rudolf Arnheim, *Art and Visual Perception: A Psychology of the Creative Eye* (Los Angeles: University of California Press, 1969), p. 351.
9. David Adams, "Rudolf Steiner's First Goetheanum as an Illustration of Organic Functionalism," *Journal of the Society of Architectural Historians* 51, no. 2 (June 1992): 190.
10. Ibid., 190.
11. Ibid., 189.

ERNSTING'S WAREHOUSE

Coesfeld, Germany 1983–85

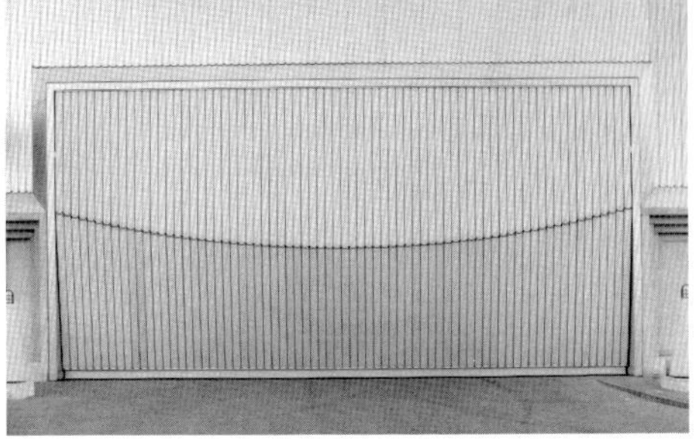

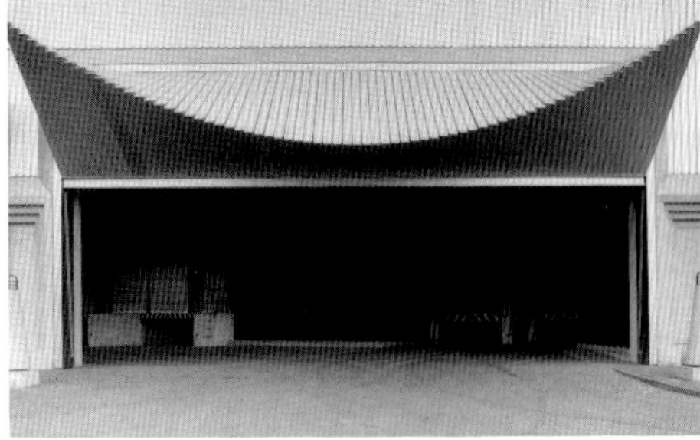

In collaboration with Bruno Reichlin and Fabio Reinhart, Calatrava won a competition to design four façades for existing industrial structures. Each of the façades represents a different application of aluminum: waves of corrugated aluminum in the long wall of the warehouse, slats of aluminum for the warehouse doors, a window shaped like a bellows camera on the south elevation, and an arched bridge that connects the old and new buildings. The entire structure becomes a study in light, material, movement, and three-dimensional form.

Detail of warehouse door

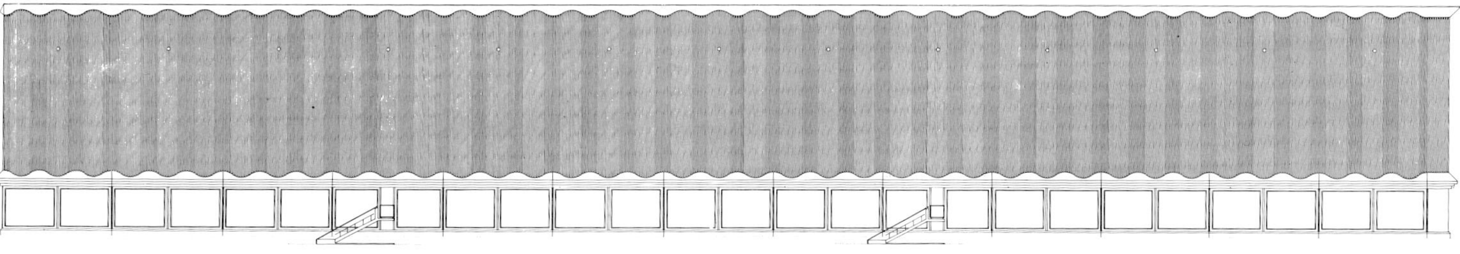

Elevation

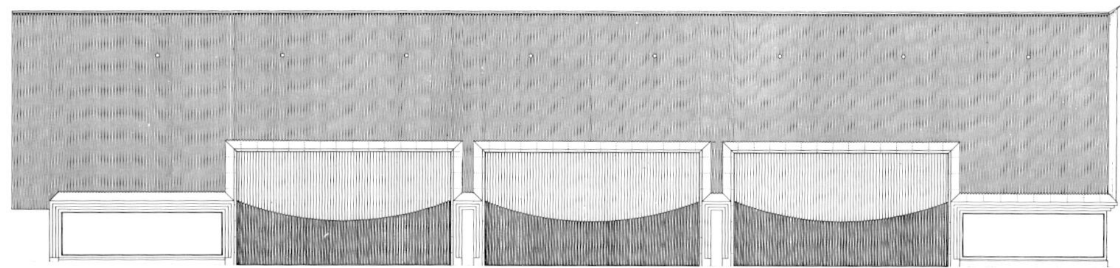

Elevation

Elevation

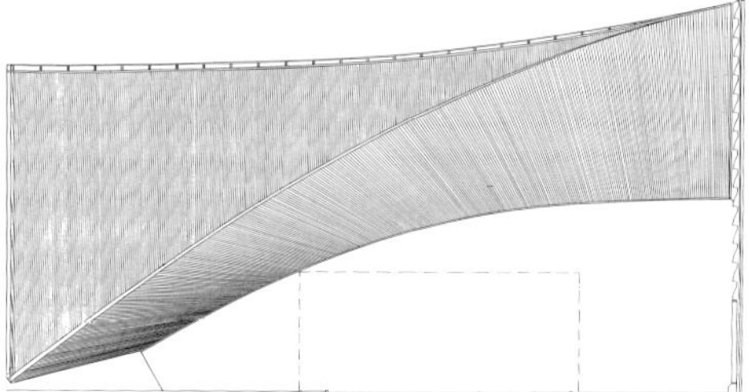

Bridge

KUWAIT PAVILION, 1992 WORLD'S FAIR

Seville 1991–92

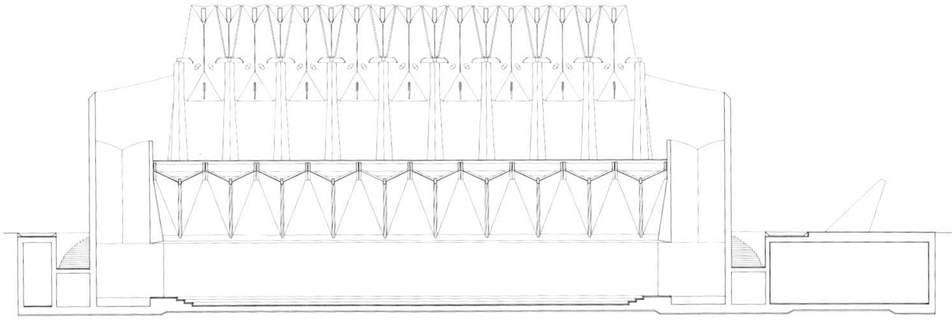

Longitudinal section

This pavilion, commissioned by the Government of Kuwait, is the third in a series of structures in which Calatrava explores a roof that can open and close. Whereas Calatrava's Swissbau Pavilion and his proposed pavilion on the Lake of Lucerne are made out of concrete, he made the moving components in the Kuwait Pavilion out of wood. These ribs are arranged in two rows, one of eight and one of nine, that pivot on a tubular rail that is connected to the concrete bases. The ribs can be maneuvered from a 45-degree resting position up to 90 degrees and seem to be abstractions of palm fronds that gently fan visitors, providing relief from the sun.

The pavilion itself is set on a platform partially comprised of marble-glass laminate panels that glow at night, illuminated by the lighted exhibition gallery below.

Right: Section

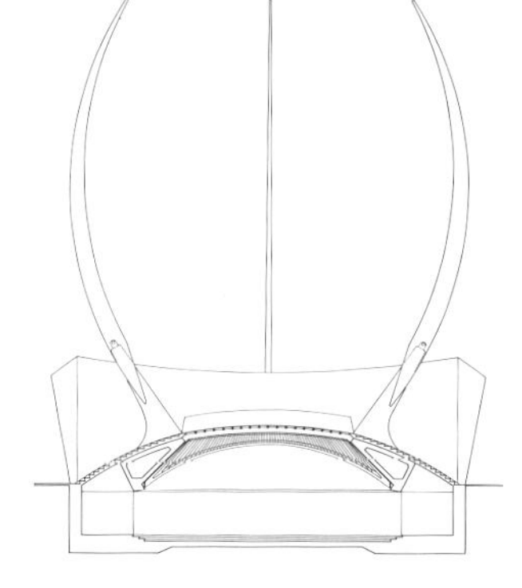

Below right: Preliminary sketches. Section

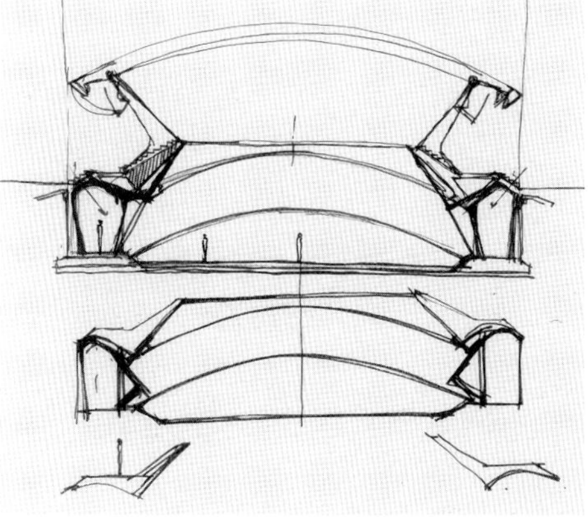

Preliminary sketch. Plan

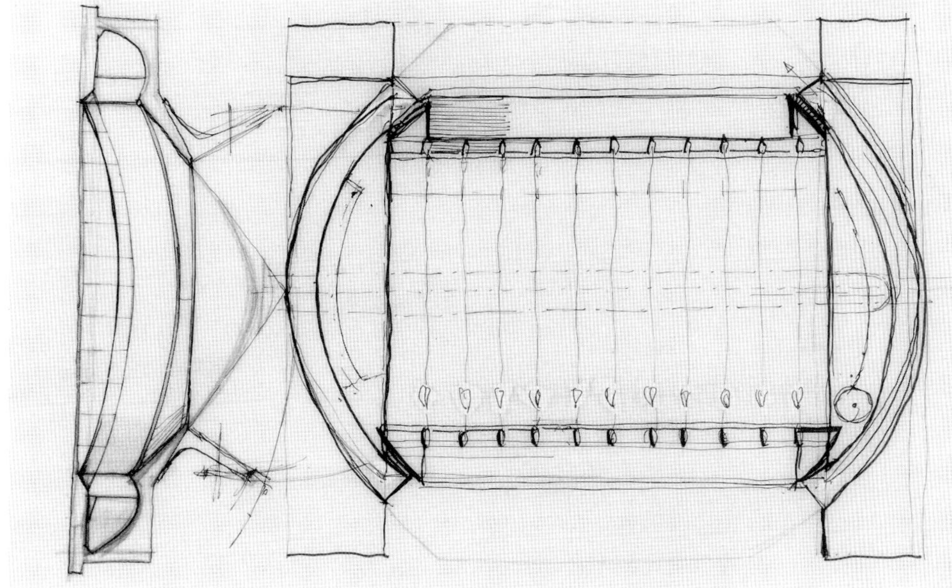

LYONS AIRPORT RAILROAD STATION

Lyons-Satolas 1989–

In preparation for the 1992 Winter Olympics in Albertville, an extension was proposed for the French high-speed train network (TGV) that would connect its line between Paris and Marseilles with the Lyons airport. Although only the tracks and train platform were expected to be completed in time for the Olympics, Calatrava's winning entry, currently under construction, also includes a station hall, a connecting gallery to the airport, and a new TGV station.

A 500-meter-long (1,640-foot-long) vaulted roof covers the tracks and the roadway above them, revealing a beautiful lattice arrangement of concrete ribs. This pattern is repeated on a smaller scale in steel in the connecting gallery to the airport. The station hall, the last of the structures to be completed, will be built out of steel clad in aluminum, and its form will embody the idea of flight and passage.

Longitudinal section (view from the west), competition entry

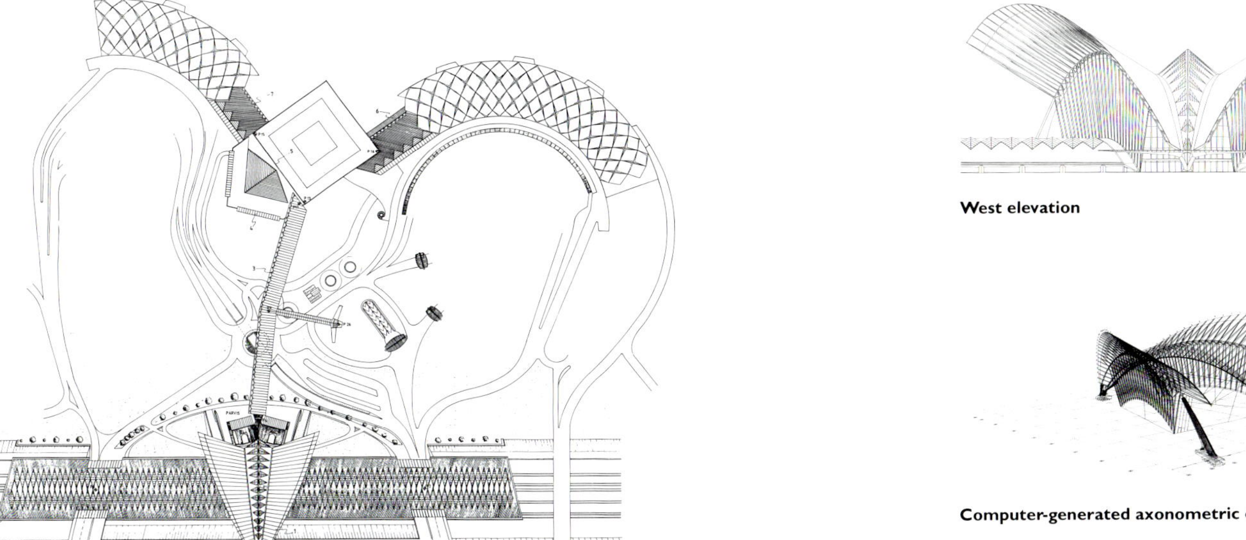

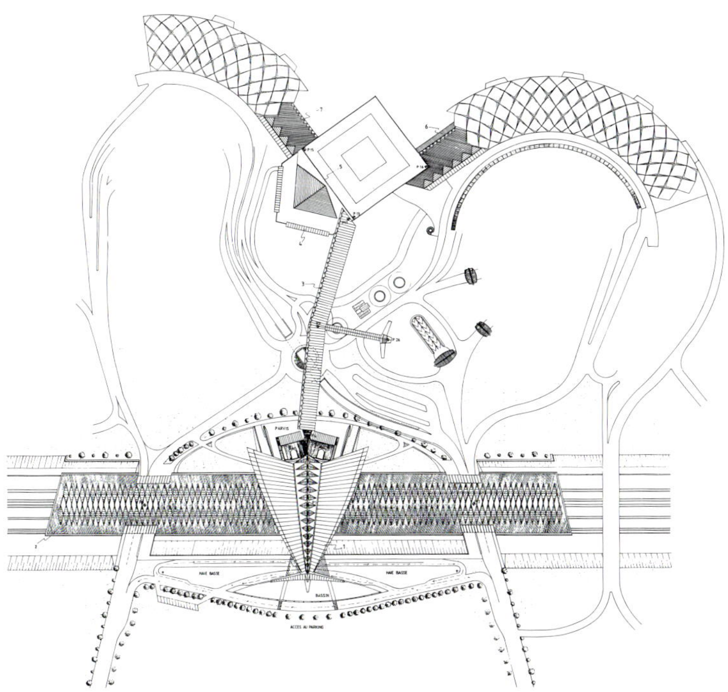

Site plan

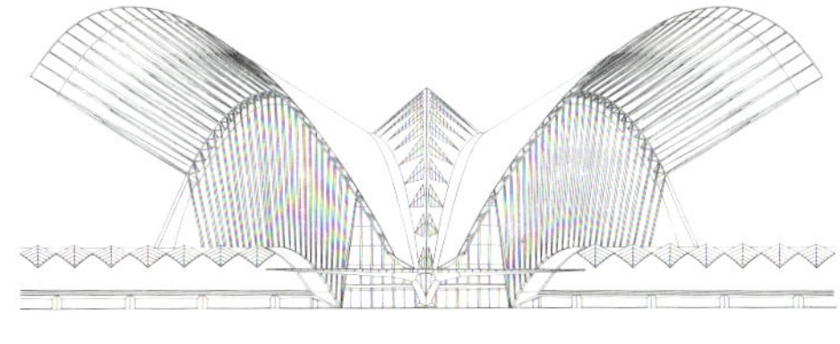

West elevation

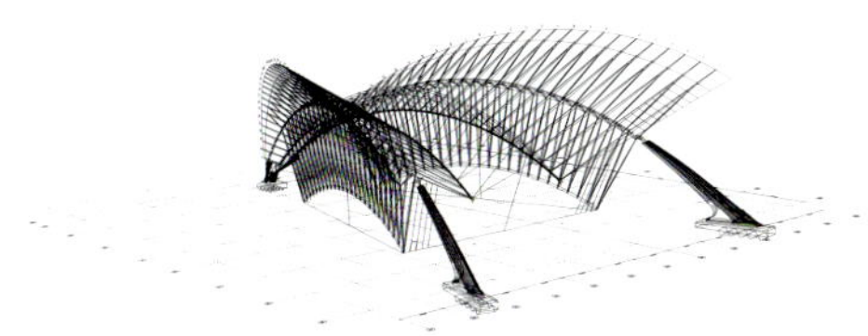

Computer-generated axonometric of station hall

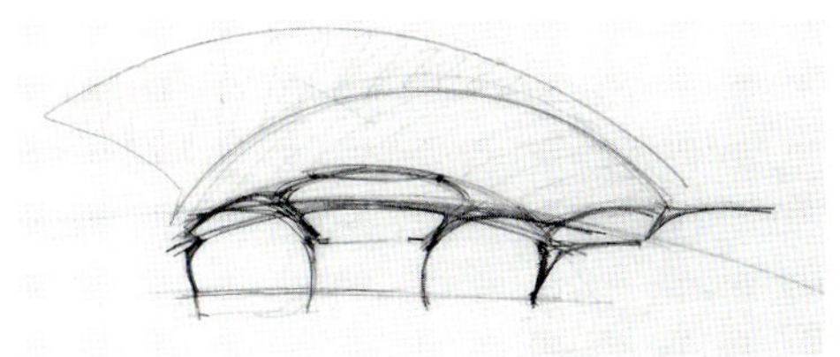

Preliminary sketch. Section through platform

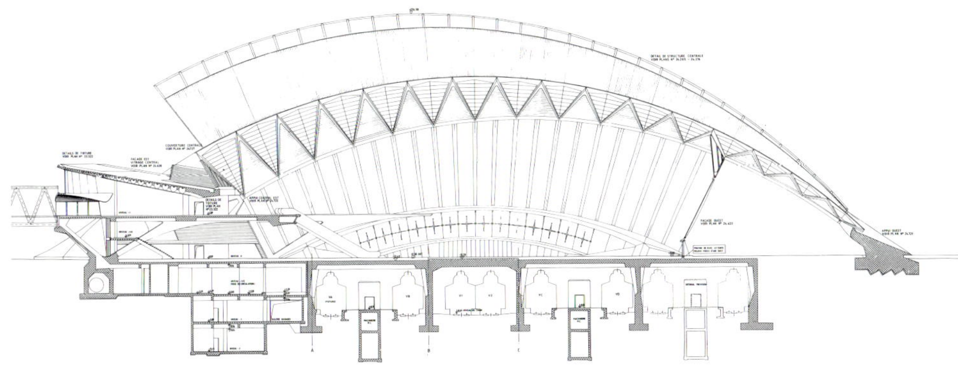

Section of station hall

Longitudinal section (view from the east), competition entry

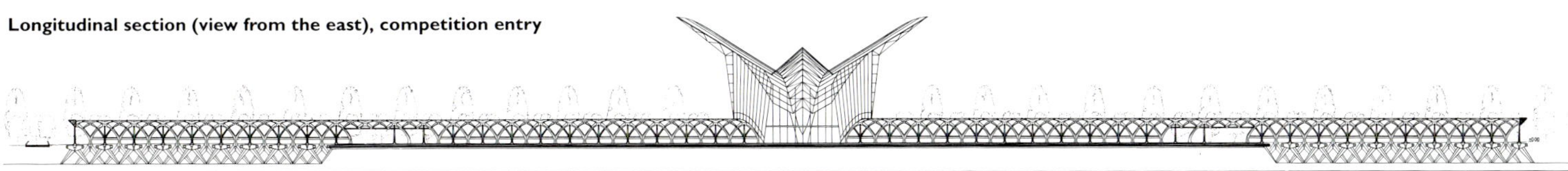

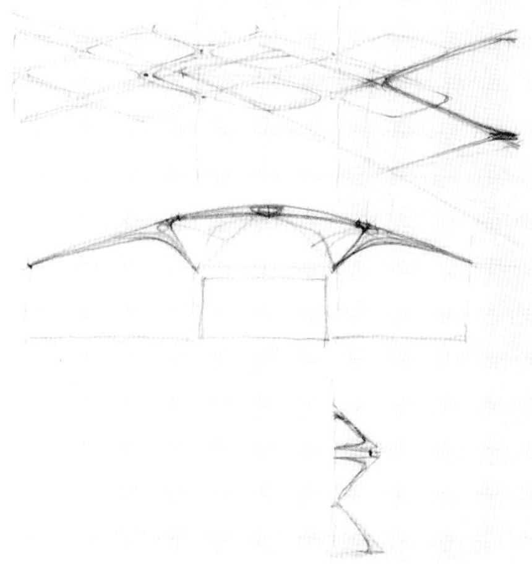

Preliminary sketches. Platform roof structure and cross section through platforms

Passageway to platforms

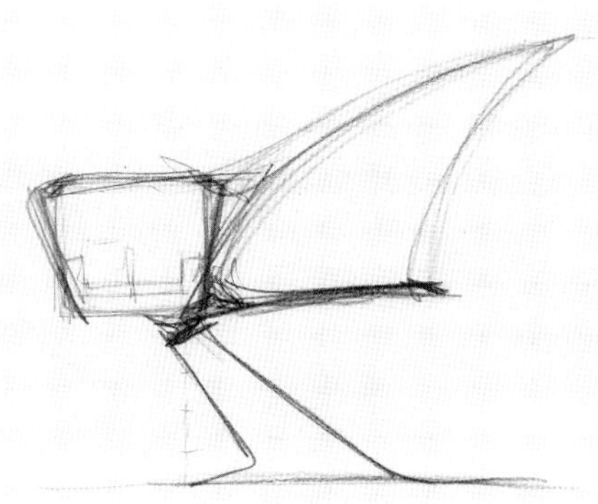

Preliminary sketch. Connecting gallery to airport terminal

Preliminary sketches for station hall

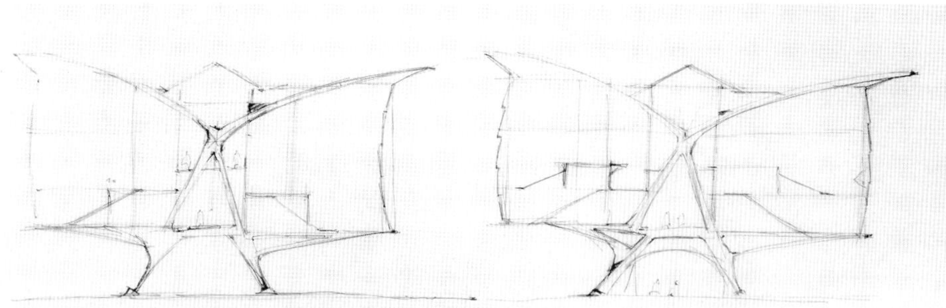

Detail of platform roof

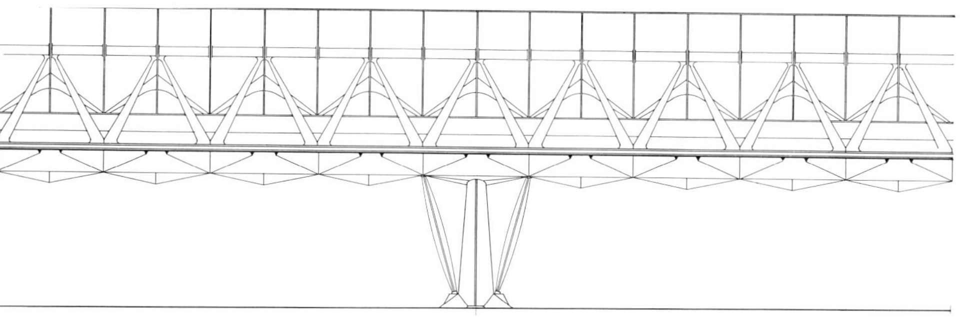

Longitudinal section of connecting gallery (view from the south)

Connecting gallery

STADELHOFEN RAILROAD STATION

Zurich 1983–90

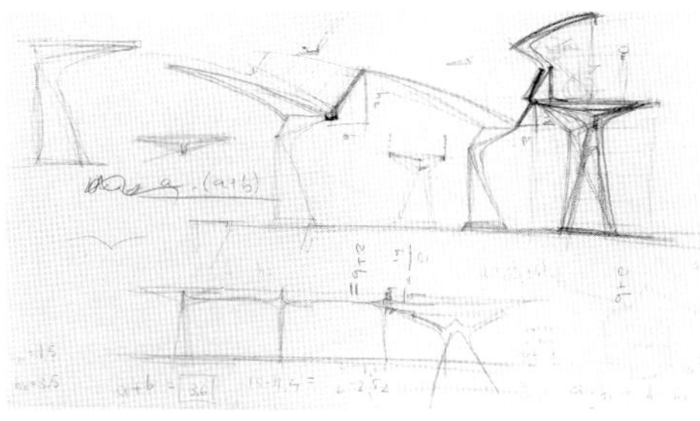

Preliminary sketches. Entrance canopy to underpass

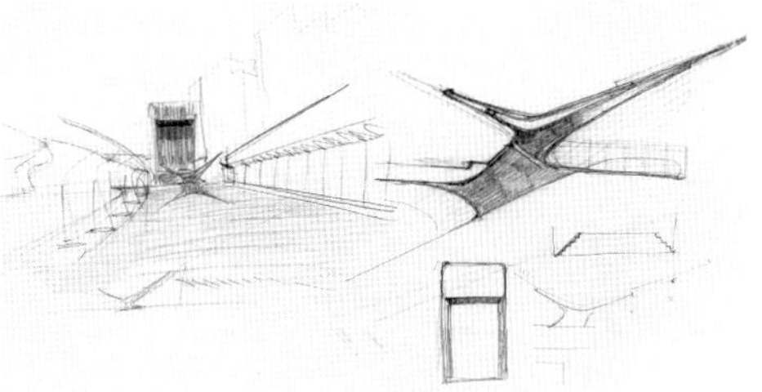

Preliminary sketches. Train platform and entrance to underpass

Sketch of platform, glass canopy, and promenade with footbridge (Falkensteg) in foreground

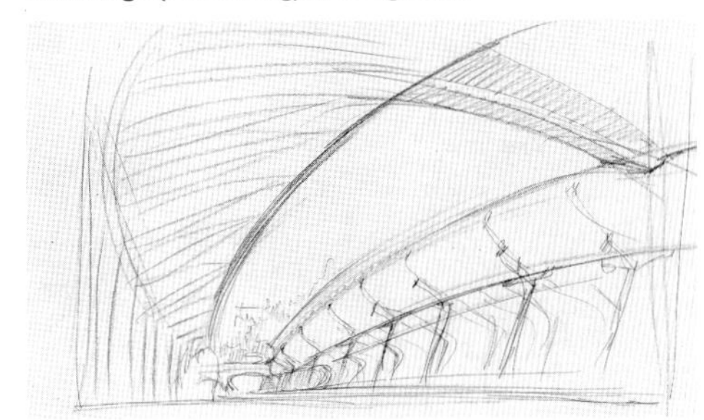

Section through footbridge (Falkensteg)

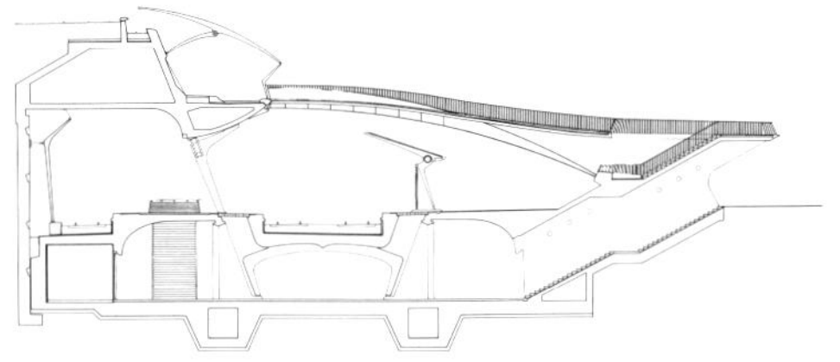

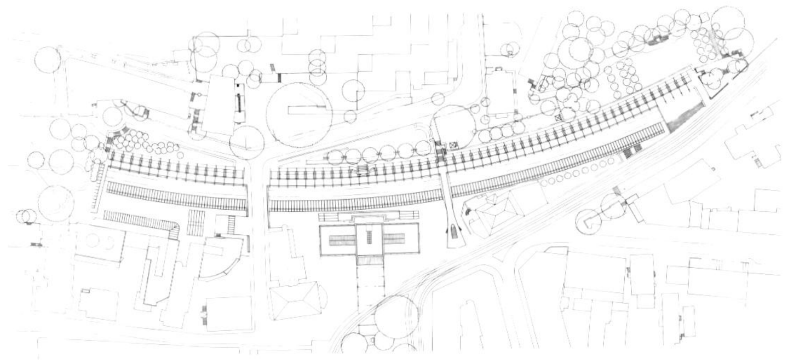

Site plan

Lower commercial level and subway connecting element between platforms

Promenade

In collaboration with Arnold Amsler and Werner Rueger, Calatrava had the winning entry in a competition to remodel and add to Stadelhofen Railroad Station.

Situated at the foot of a park-like hill that was once the limit of the old fortified city, Calatrava's three-part station is integrated by the repetition of distinctive constructive elements. A promenade above the train platform includes a series of light steel structures forming a pergola that will eventually have a canopy of greenery above and cascading over the walls. The 270-meter-long (886-foot-long) train platform below consists of repeated tripartite Y-shaped columns that support either glass or concrete canopies for each of the three tracks. The commercial level underneath exploits the sculptural quality of concrete and resembles a large ribcage. Natural daylight penetrates to this level from strips of glass block in the sidewalks of the station platform above.

The station itself bridges parts of Zurich—the Opera House square and the hillside neighborhood above the station. Stadelhofen is an urban insertion that functions not only as a train station but as an extension of its immediate surroundings.

View of footbridge (Falkensteg)

Elevation and section

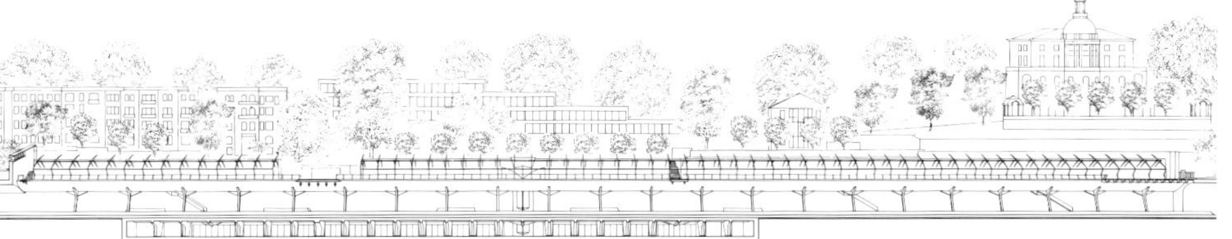

SPANDAU RAILROAD STATION (PROJECT)

Berlin 1991

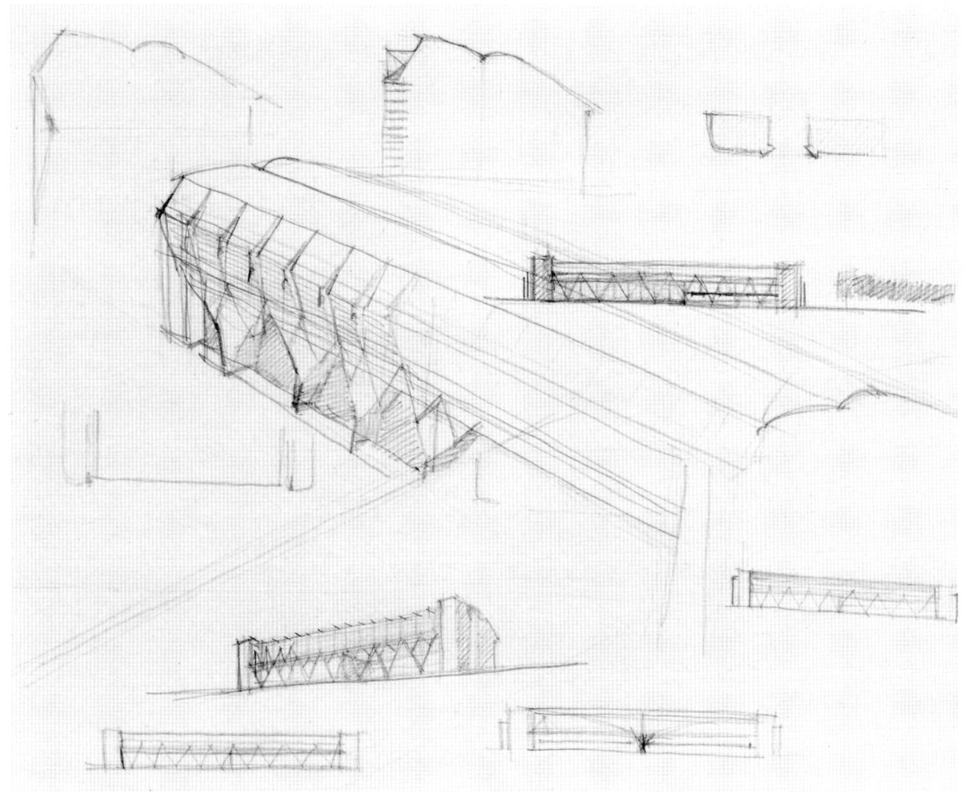

Sketches. Studies for commercial blocks

In a two-stage international competition for the design of a major railroad station in the northeast part of Berlin, Calatrava's winning scheme involved a central station suspended between two proposed larger commercial blocks. The trains run through the buildings and underneath tree-like structures that support the glass canopy above. With these elements Calatrava creates a unified urban composition transporting the public park into the train station itself. The extension of the city and creation of open city spaces that began with Stadelhofen take place on a larger scale in Spandau. Both projects illustrate Calatrava's ability to give each location a distinctive and new identity.

Longitudinal section through the station

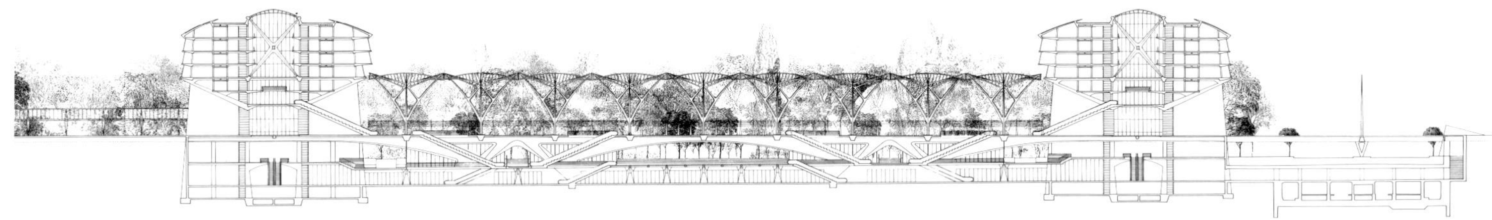

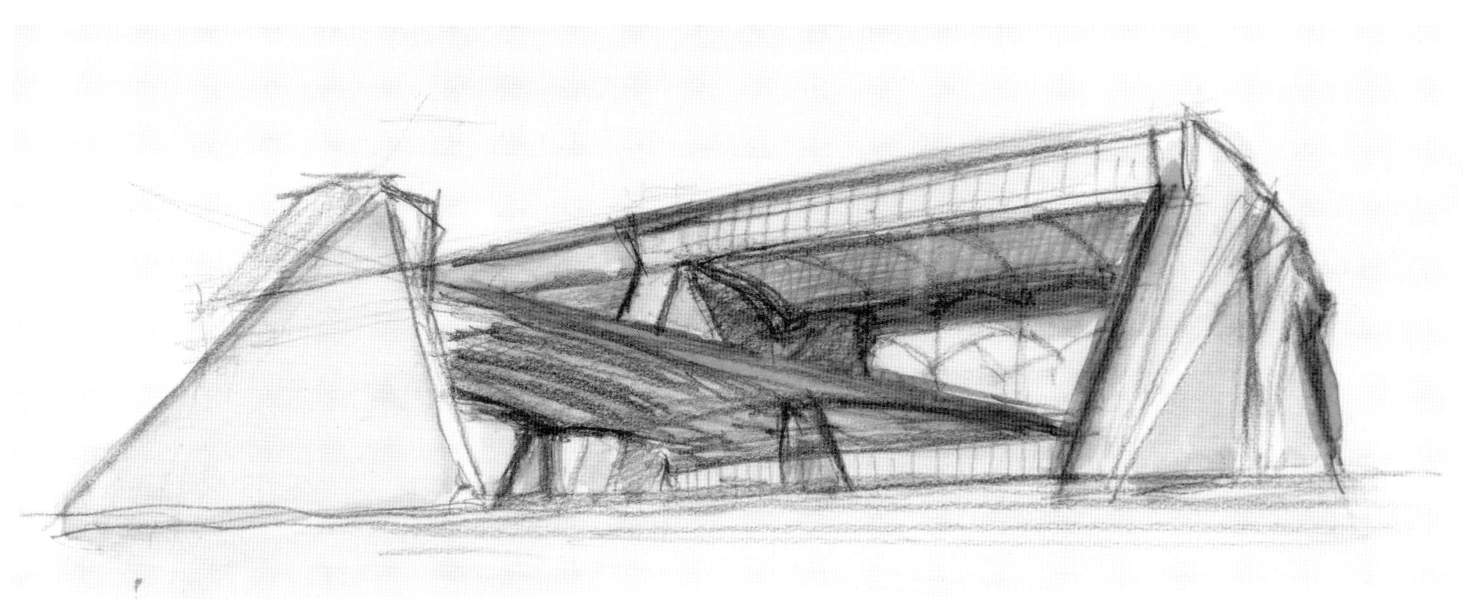

Sketch. Proposed commercial block with train tracks passing through

Site plan

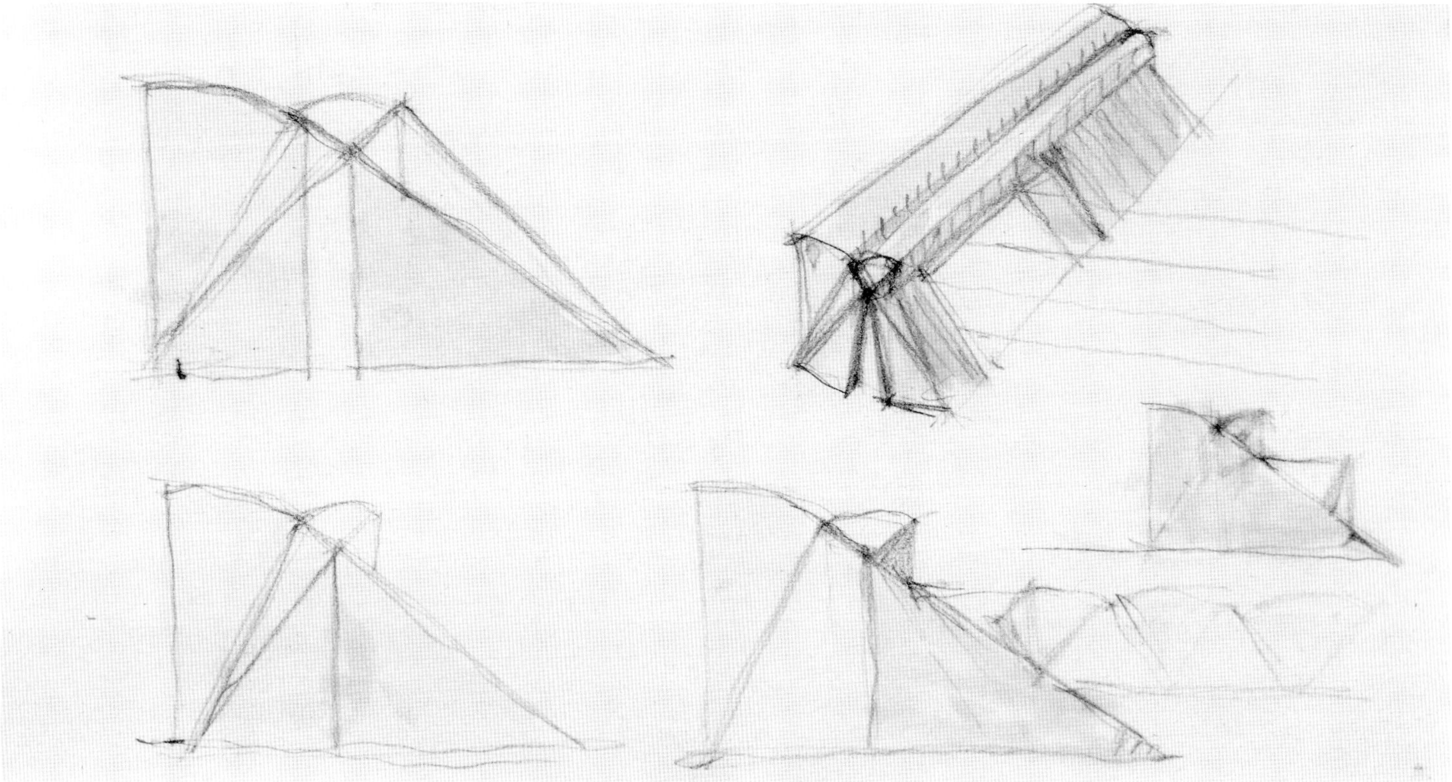

Sketches. Studies for commercial block

Cross section through railroad station showing idea of park to the left and right

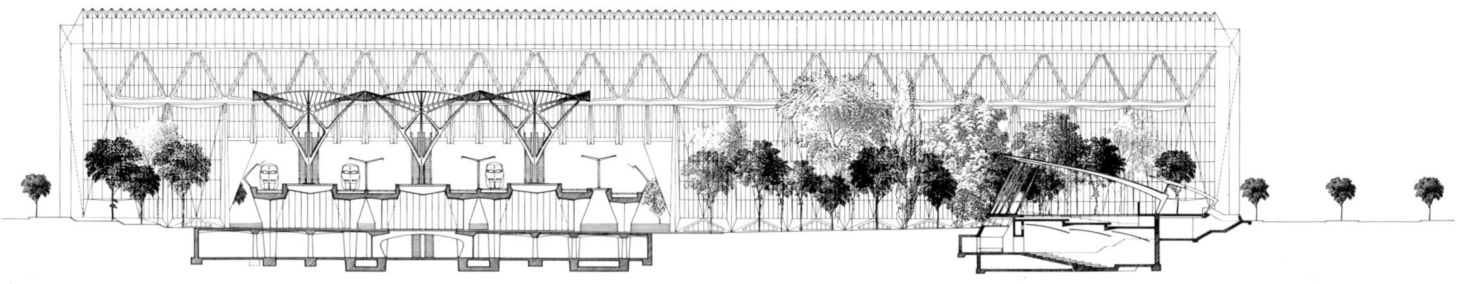

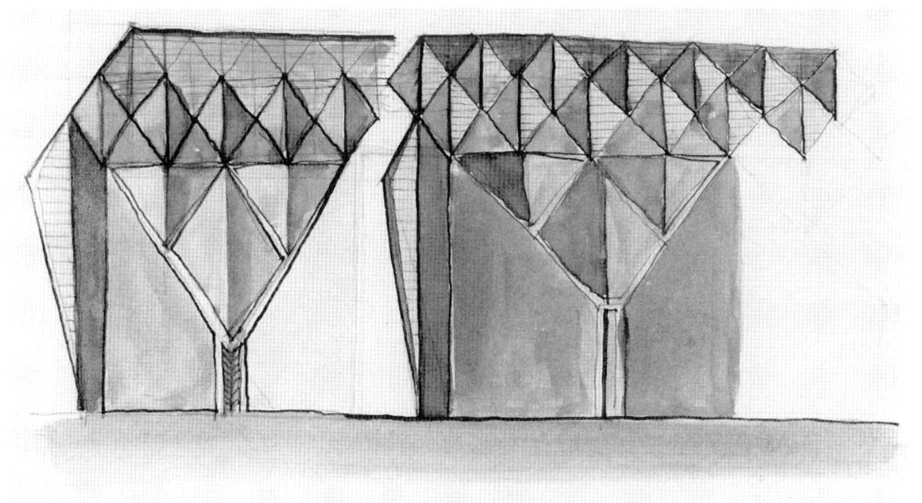

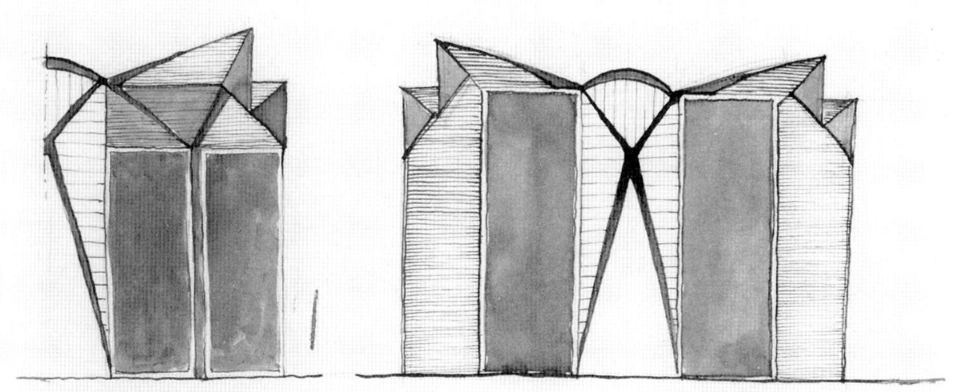

Sketches. Studies for commercial blocks

Section and elevation

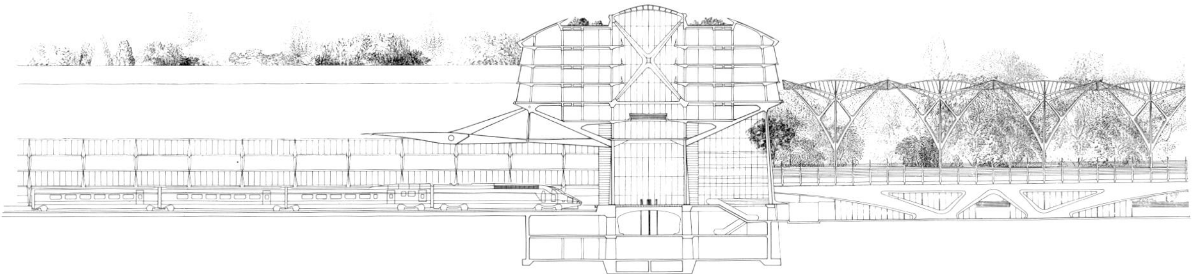

CATHEDRAL OF SAINT JOHN THE DIVINE, RENÉ DUBOS BIOSHELTER (PROJECT)

New York City 1991–

The competition for a design to complete the north and south transepts of the Cathedral of Saint John the Divine in New York City required a bioshelter to be included in the design. Nancy Jack and John Todd, biologists and cathedral colleagues, defined "bioshelter" as follows: "A solar-age workhorse that integrates architecture with food production, water purification, and recycling of wastes, and blends structure, living systems, and solar and electronic technologies to support human culture within a sustainable ecology." Using the image of a tree as the basic element of composition, Calatrava's bioshelter is successfully integrated into the cathedral's Gothic setting and follows its cross-plan. The bioshelter's placement directly under the roof and in the attic of the present nave dictates that the cathedral will have a new, glazed roof.

Important design issues that Calatrava considered include the use of stone as the structural material and the ways in which light filters through the trees above the nave and transept. Just as the cathedral perceives itself to be a microcosm of the city, so Calatrava's addition extends the cathedral's architecture as well as its spiritual and ecological ideals.

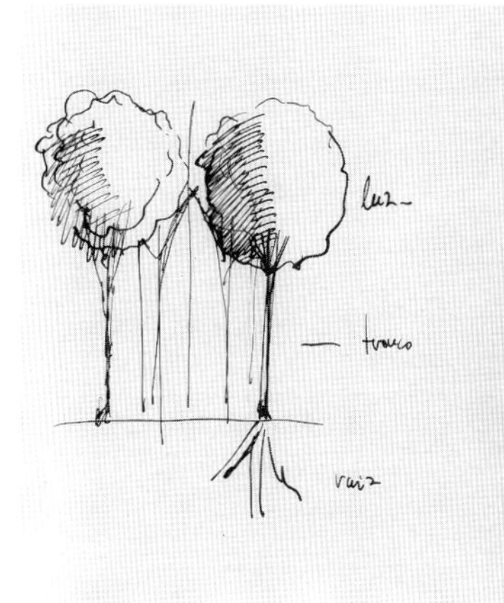

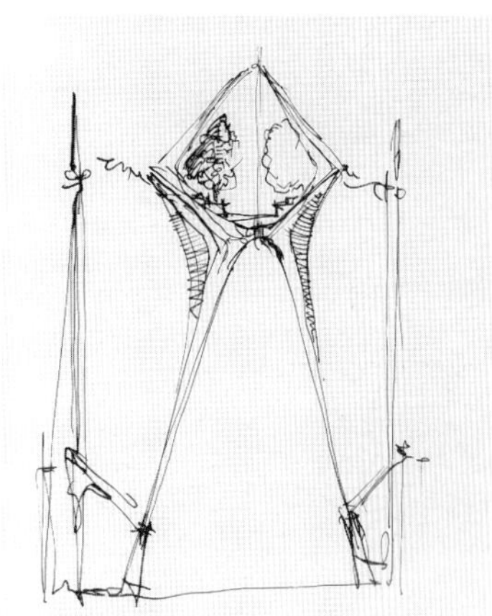

Site plan

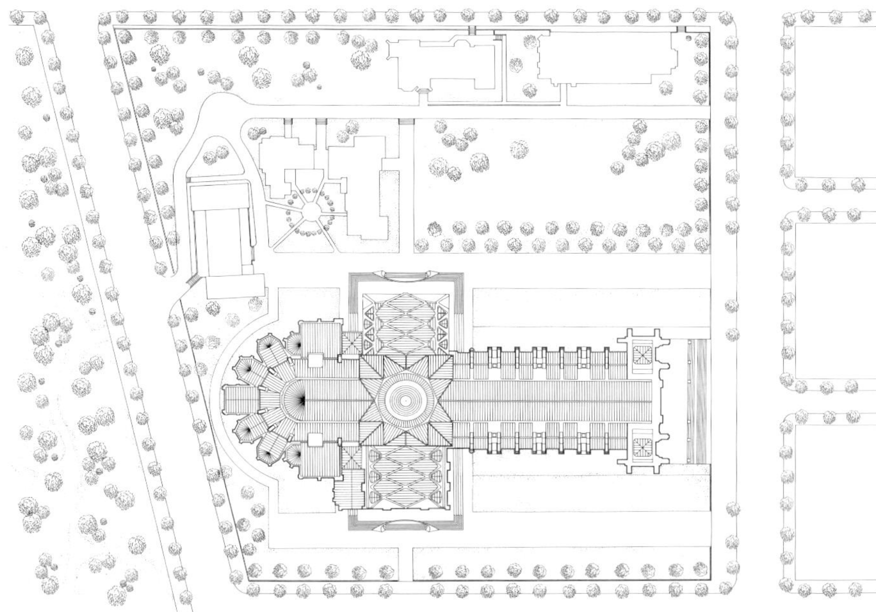

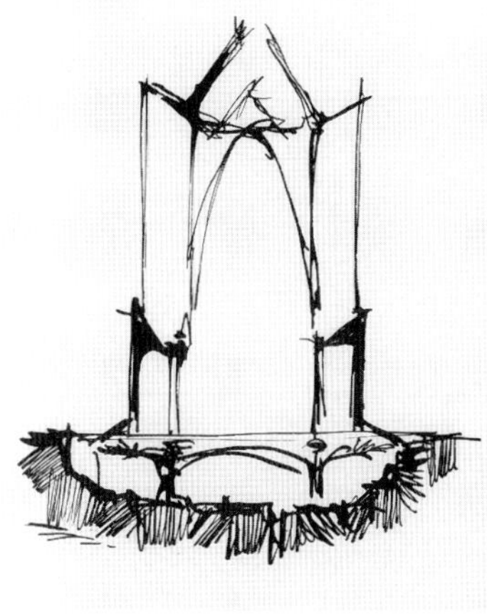
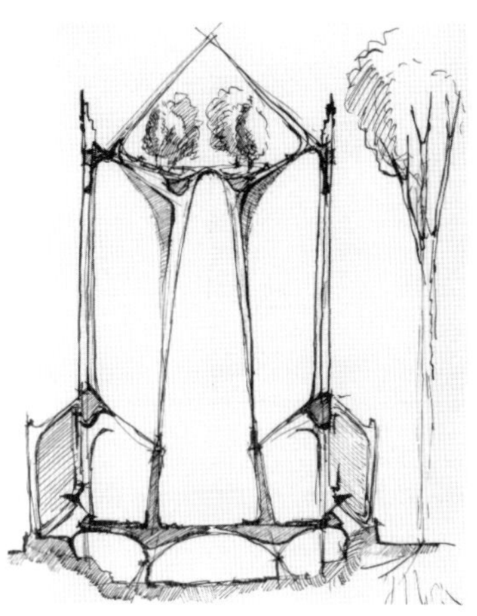
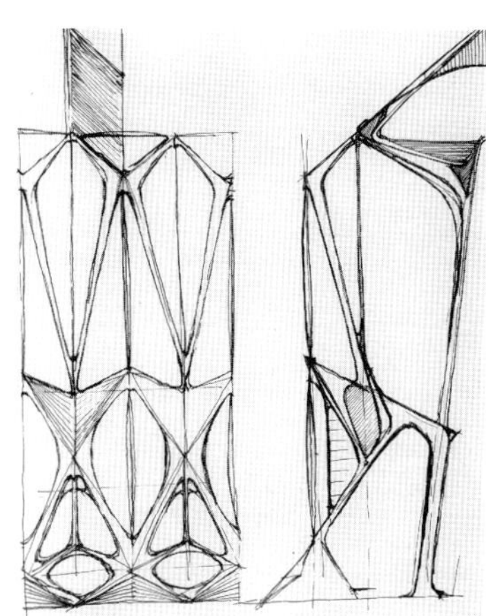
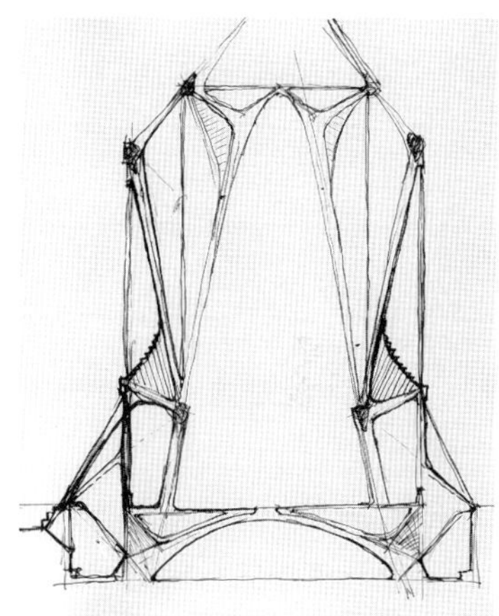

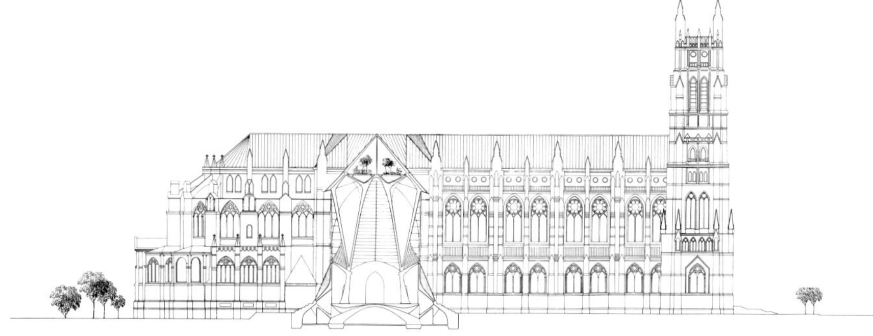

Section of south transept

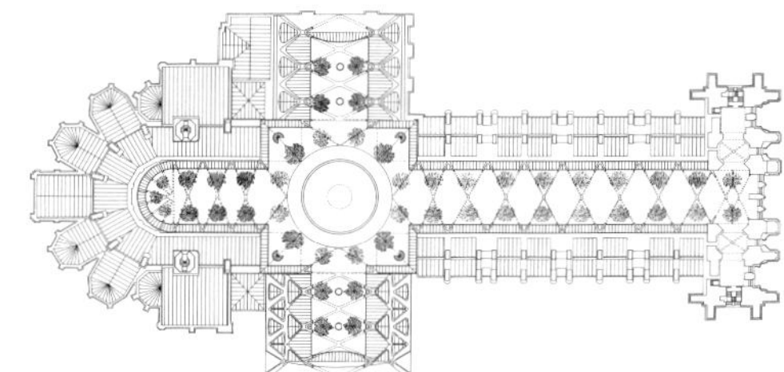

Plan of bioshelter

Longitudinal section along the central axis

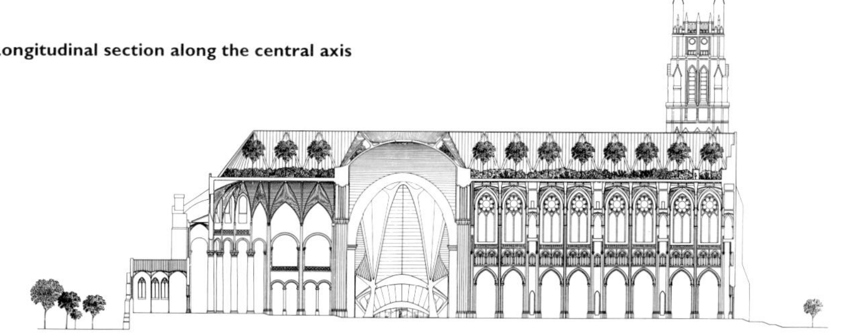

SCIENCE MUSEUM, PLANETARIUM, AND TELECOMMUNICATIONS TOWER

Valencia 1991–

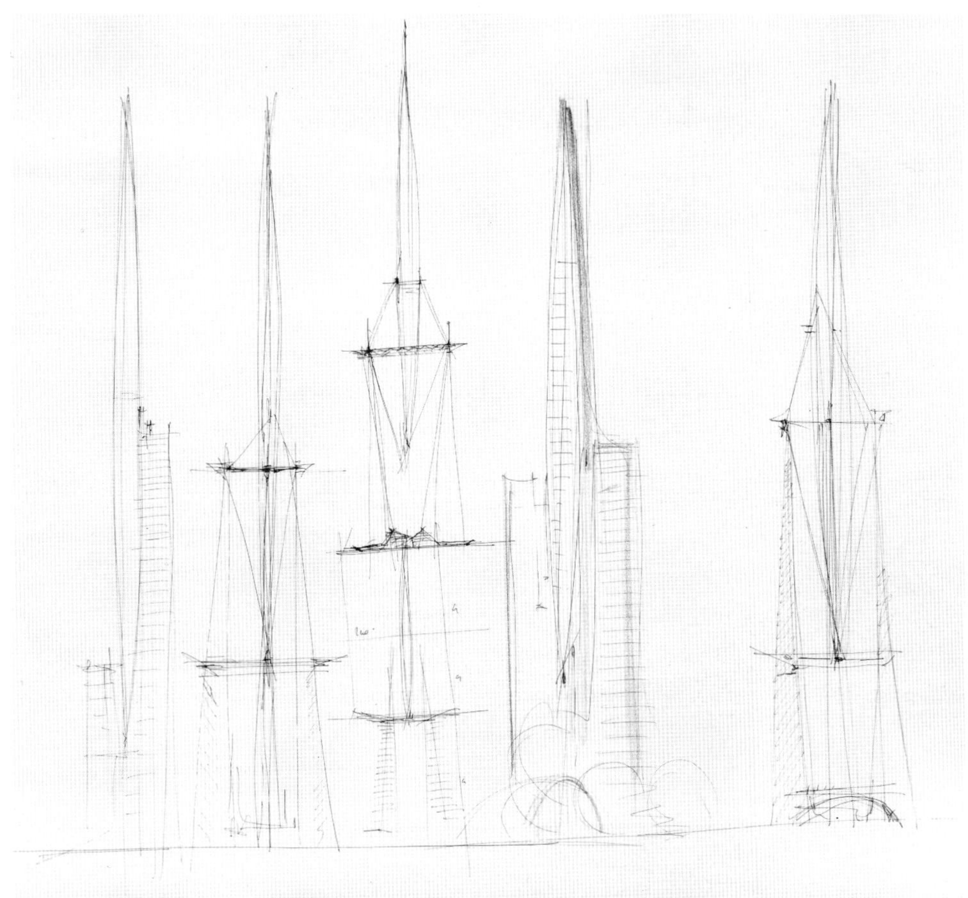

Telecommunications Tower. Preliminary sketches

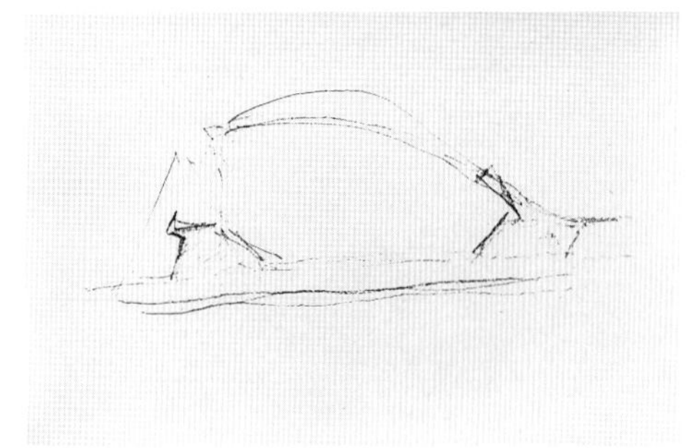

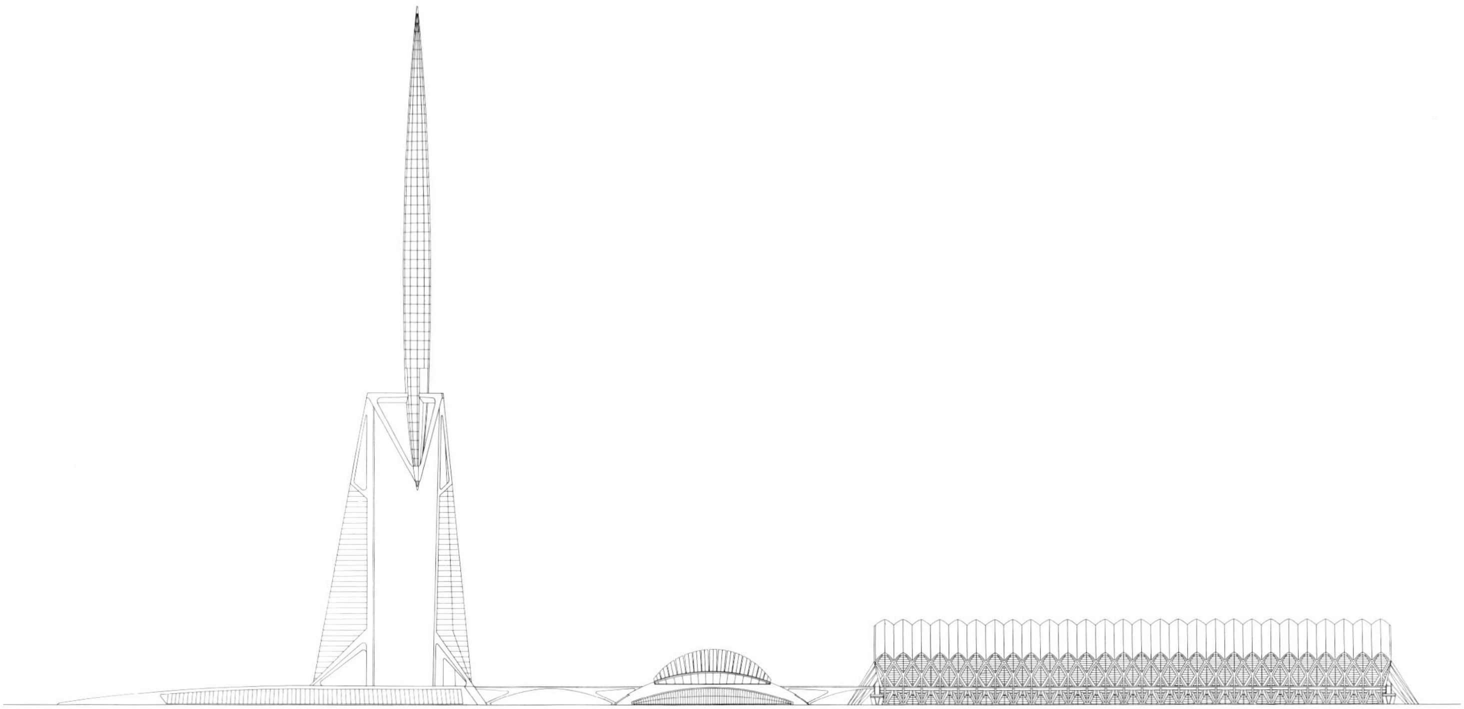

South elevation

Science Museum. Preliminary sketches of plan and elevation

This proposed complex of three buildings—the winning entry in a design competition—is located on an eye-shaped site beside the Turia riverbed, east of the old city center. The buildings are ordered around an elevated central walkway that links, at one end, Calatrava's 327-meter-high (1,073-foot-high) Telecommunications Tower with the long-ribbed Science Museum at the other. In the middle is an elliptical structure that houses a planetarium above and a library, auditoria, and restaurants below. Similar to the roof of the Kuwait Pavilion in that it moves, the Planetarium roof opens and closes, offering views of the sky.

Like many of Calatrava's other urban structures, the Tower serves more than one purpose: it functions as a communications center but also creates a landmark for both the site and the city. The sectional drawings of the Science Museum, resembling the natural image of the charging bull, offer a counterpoint to this monument to telecommunications. The main exhibition hall of the museum includes dramatic balconies that run the length of the museum on the north and south sides. The drawing of the site elevation reveals a rich and diverse sequence of buildings that collectively are devoted to the celebration of science.

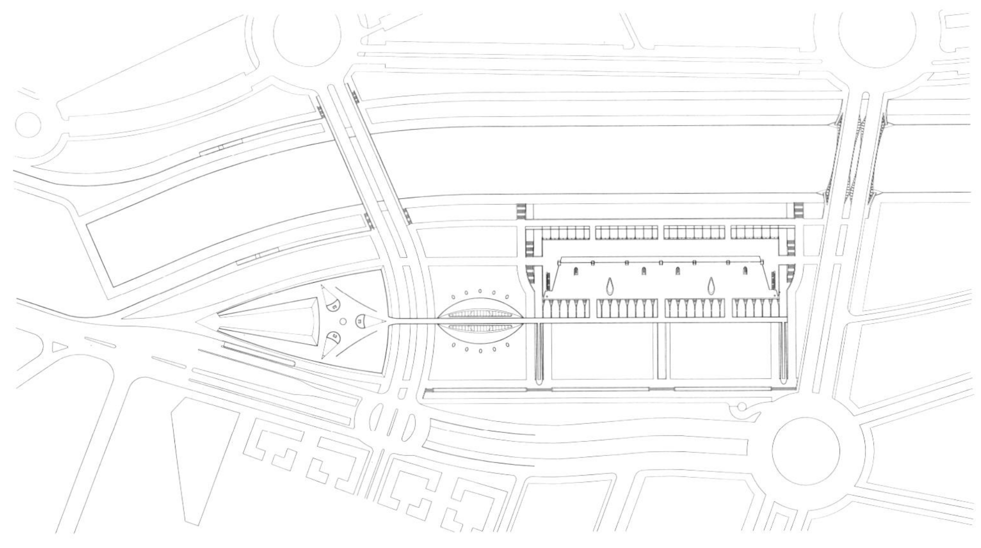

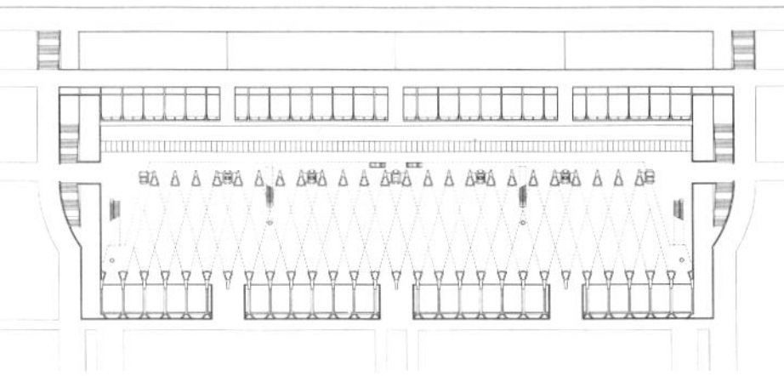

Science Museum. First floor plan

Site plan

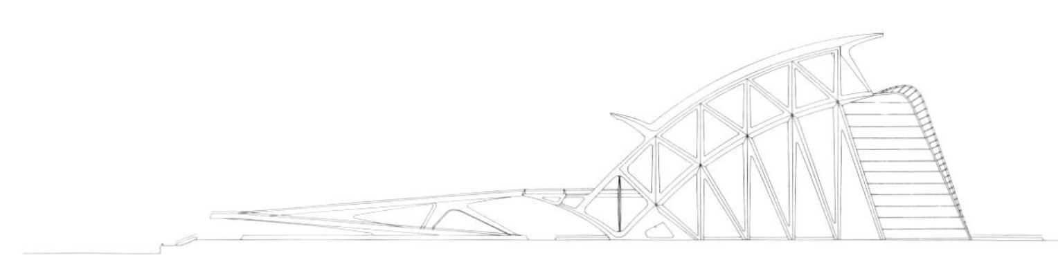

East elevation

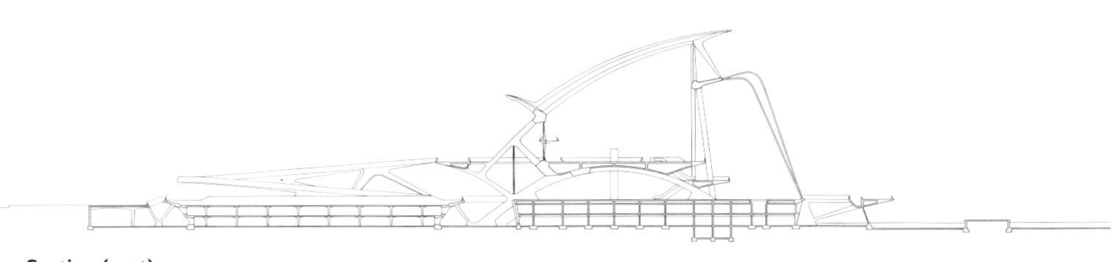

Section (east)

Science Museum. North elevation

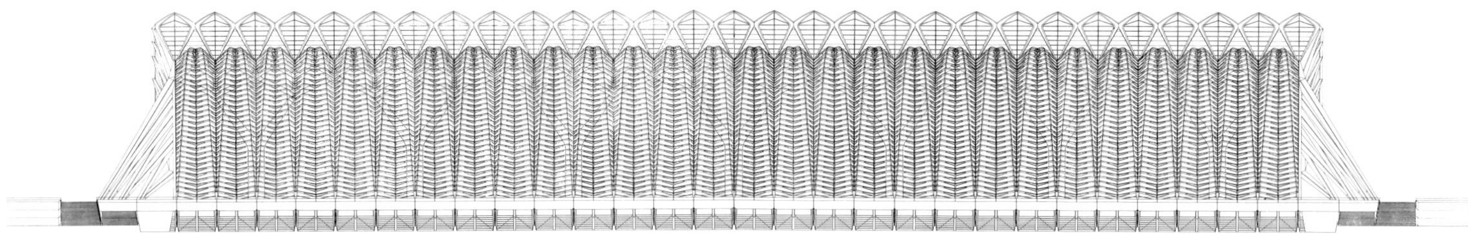

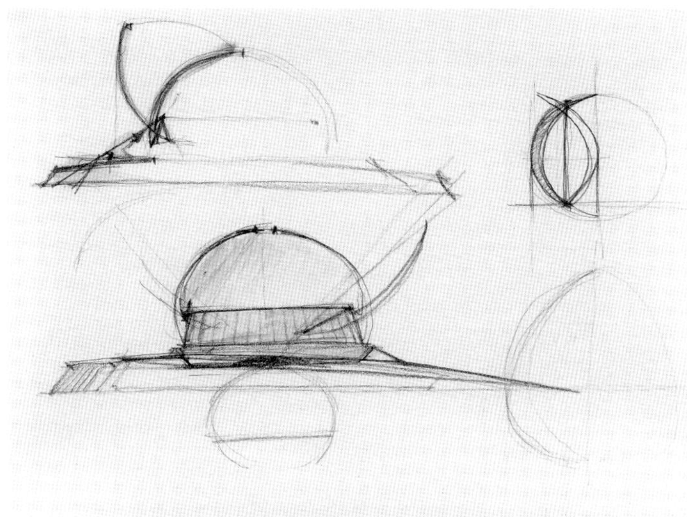

Planetarium. Preliminary sketches

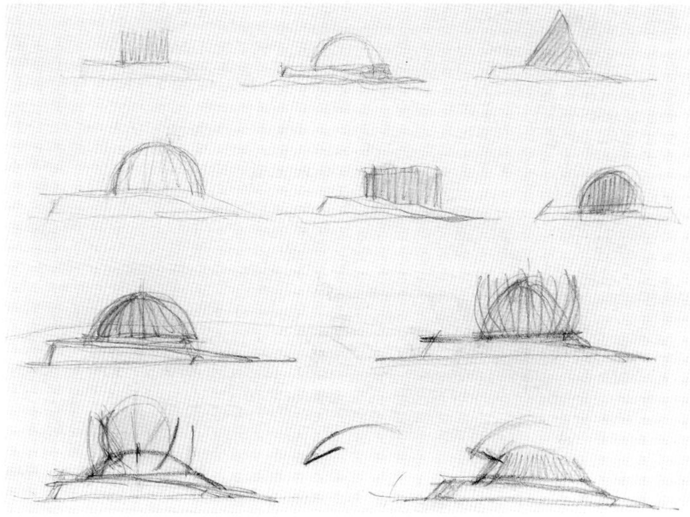

Planetarium. Preliminary sketches

Science Museum. Preliminary sketch of section

Science Museum. Longitudinal section

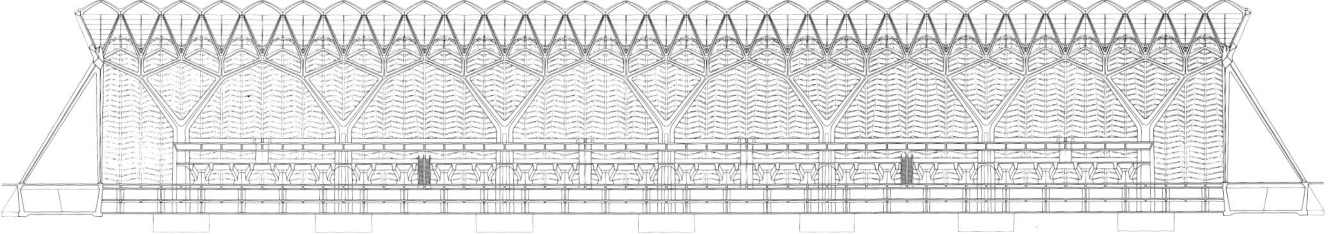

BACH DE RODA – FELIPE II BRIDGE

Barcelona 1984–87

As part of a plan to revitalize certain Barcelona neighborhoods on the occasion of the 1992 Olympics, the Unitat Operativa de Projectes Urbans, Servei de Projectes d'Element Urbans, commissioned Calatrava to build a bridge that is a new traffic and pedestrian connection between the areas of Sant Andrea and San Marti. The bridge has a total length of 140 meters (459 feet) and spans 68 meters (226 feet). It is comprised of two pairs of steel arches from which a roadway and sidewalks are suspended by pairs of cables. Following the curve of the outside canted arches, stairways descend to park grounds. Roadway lights are incorporated into the middle of the bridge, while footpaths are illuminated by strip-lighting integrated into the handrails. One of his most important early commissions, Calatrava's bridge becomes at once a gateway, urban plaza, and focal point for what will be one of the largest green areas in the city.

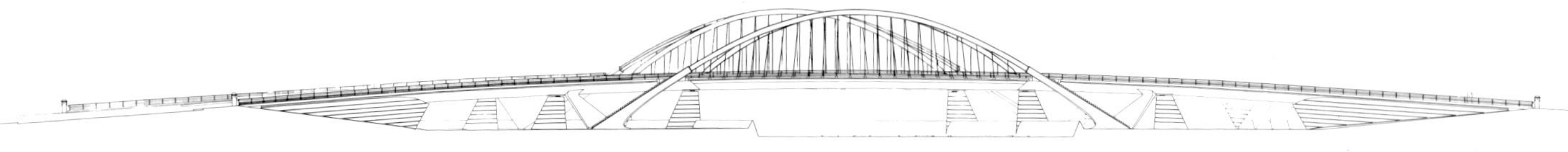

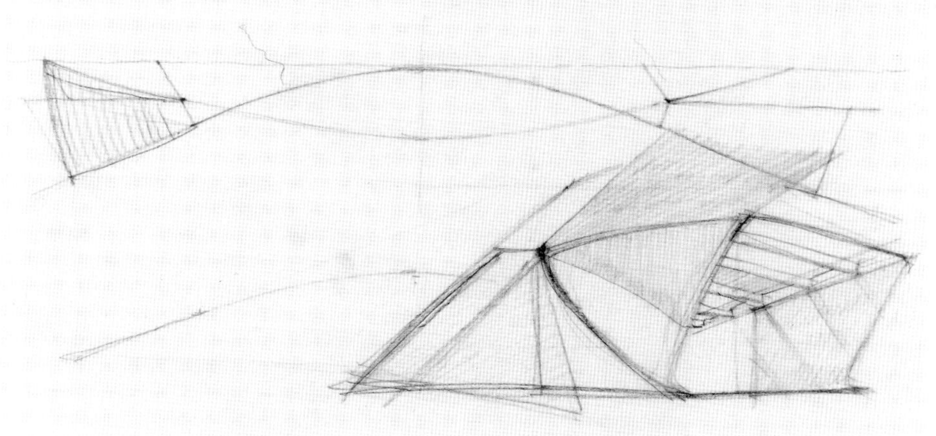

Preliminary sketch. Concrete form underneath bridge

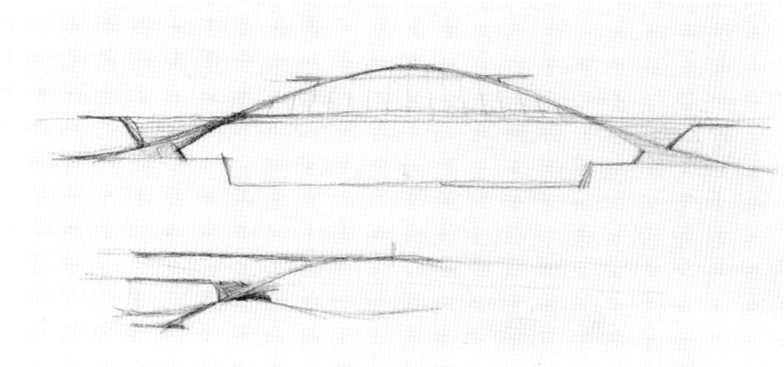

Preliminary form-finding sketches

Underside of bridge during construction

Site plan

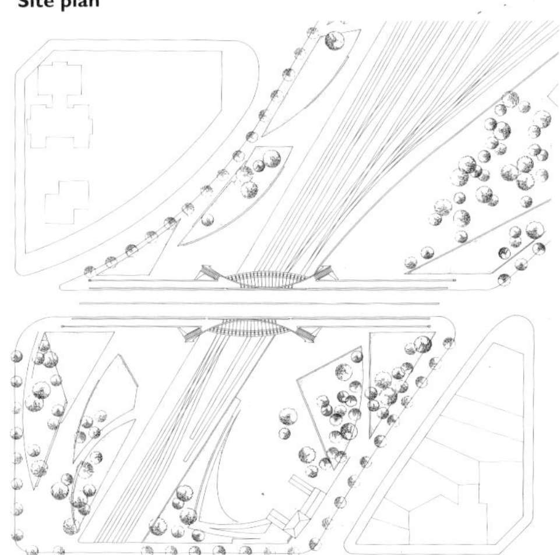

Cross section before stairs

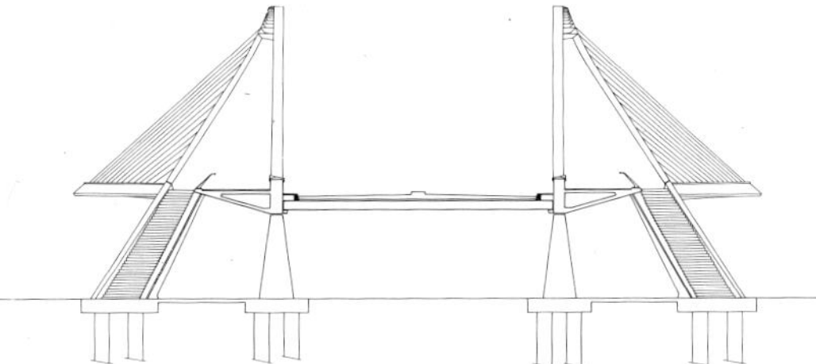

ALAMILLO BRIDGE AND CARTUGA VIADUCT

Seville 1987–92

Commissioned by La Junta de Andalusia as part of civic improvements planned to coincide with the 1992 World's Fair, Expo '92, the Alamillo Bridge, 200 meters (656 feet) long, spans the Meandro San Jeronimo. The 500-meter-long (1,641-foot-long) Cartuga Viaduct acted as a gateway to the north entrance of the Expo site. Like Calatrava's Telecommunications Tower for Valencia, his bridge and viaduct are both landmark and monument.

The bridge deck consists of a hexagonal steel box beam to which thirteen pairs of steel cable stays are attached. The weight of the concrete-filled steel pylon, which rises 142 meters (466 feet), supports the deck and contains a service stair to the top. Two traffic decks cantilever off the box beam; above them are an elevated pedestrian and bicycle path in the tradition of the Brooklyn Bridge.

The original scheme included two symmetrical bridges one and a half kilometers (4,921 feet) apart that would be angled toward each other, creating a symmetrical composition. For political reasons this scheme was abandoned in favor of one bridge, which possibly is stronger for its singularity and asymmetry.

Preliminary sketches

A street lamp on the viaduct

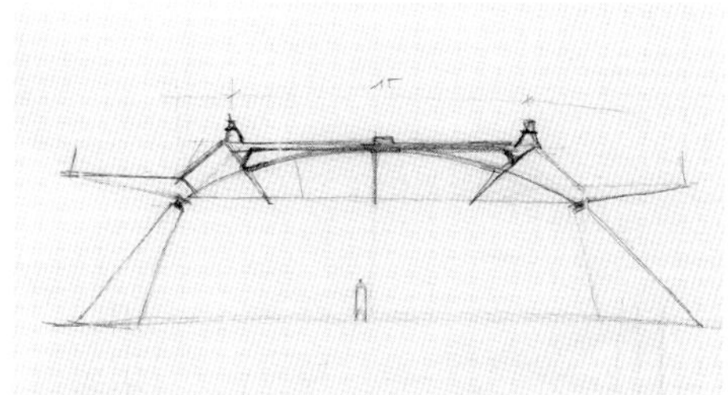

Preliminary sketch. Section of viaduct

Underside of viaduct

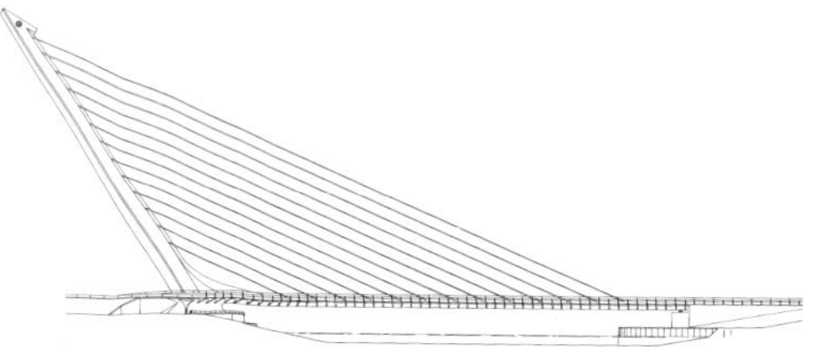

Elevation

Site plan

Cross section

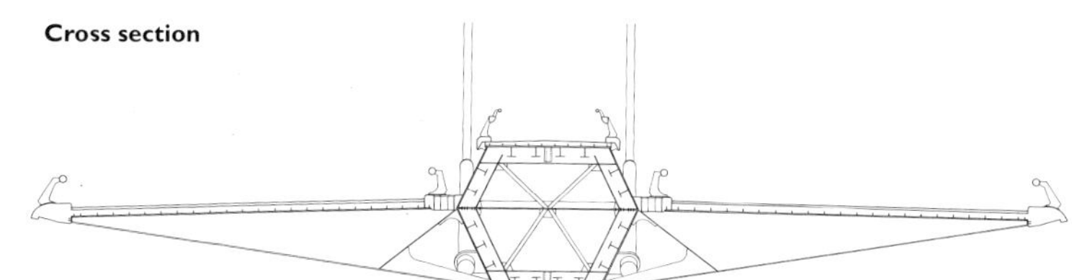

TRUSTEES OF THE MUSEUM OF MODERN ART